Legal Almanac Series No. 82

OBSCENITY AND PORNOGRAPHY

The Law Under the First Amendment

by DANIEL S. MORETTI

General Editor
Irving J. Sloan

1984
Oceana Publications, Inc.
London • Rome • New York

ACKNOWLEDGMENT

The author gratefully acknowledges the help of Kevin Egan, Donna German, and Regina Allegretti in writing this book.

The Legal Almanac Series brings you the law on various subjects in non-technical language. These books do not take the place of your attorney's advice, but they can introduce you to your legal rights and responsibilities.

Library of Congress Cataloging in Publication Date

Moretti, Daniel S.
Obscenity and pornography.

(Legal almanac series; no. 82)
Includes index.
1. Obscenity (Law)—United States—Popular works.
2. Pornography—United States—Popular works.
3. Freedom of the press—United States—Popular works. I. Title. II. Series.
KF9444.Z9M67 1984 344.73'0547 84-18940
ISBN 0-379-11148-9 347.304547

Manufactured in the United States of America

For Michael, Nicole, and Amanda

TABLE OF CONTENTS

PREFACE

The format of this Legal Almanac is somewhat different from most volumes in this series in that much of the text analyzes the development of case law dealing with the topic of obscenity and pornography. It is not enough simply to state the law. Understanding the law of obscenity and pornography requires something more than this. Our author, Mr. Moretti, has therefore presented here a heavier dose of vocabulary in the discussion. We are confident, however, that the reader will therefore come to understand the subject in a comprehensive manner as well as gain some insight into judicial reasoning and constitutional principles.

Irving J. Sloan
General Editor

INTRODUCTION

The First Amendment to the United States Constitution prohibits the enactment of any law abridging the freedom of speech or press. Yet in 1957 the U.S. Supreme Court decided that obscene material is an exception to the First Amendment. As a result, that material which is deemed obscene may be legally banned. Today, both the federal government and the states have enacted laws making it a criminal offense to produce, distribute, or exhibit obscene material.

Since obscene material is not protected by the First Amendment, it is crucial that judges, legislators, and citizens, be able to determine what is or is not obscene. As the reader will soon realize, defining obscenity has been, and continues to be, a most difficult task. The judicial effort to find an acceptable definition of obscenity constitutes one of the longest and most arduous struggles in the history of American jurisprudence.

For these reasons, much of this book will focus on the current definition of obscenity, how it was reached, and how it is applied. This book will also concentrate on certain areas of our society where courts have found that material need not be obscene to be prohibited. For example, photographs in adult magazines which are not obscene might very well be banned if broadcast on commercial television. However, these same pictures might not be prohibited if shown on cable television (although this may soon change). Furthermore, these same pictures could not be banned if shown in a movie theatre with an "X" rating. The net result is that obscenity law has become increasingly complex. Hopefully this book will serve to lessen the complexities of modern obscenity law for the reader.

Finally, it must be remembered that although obscenity is very similar to pornography, in the eyes of the law, these terms are not synonomous. Material which is pornographic is generally protected by the First Amendment. In most instances, only if material is first judged obscene may it be prohibited.

Chapter 1
DEFINING OBSCENITY — THE EARLY HISTORY

Much of our law has been derived from English law and obscenity is no exception. The most important English case on the subject was Regina v. Hicklin, decided in 1868. There, Lord Cockburn established a strict test for obscenity which was later adopted in the United States. The test was whether the material charged as obscene tended to deprave and corrupt those whose minds are open to such immoral influences. The Hicklin test permitted courts to view isolated passages of a book, and judge them according to their harmful effects upon the most susceptible individuals. Despite some problems, the Hicklin test soon became the cornerstone of early American obscenity law.

The Hicklin test was thoroughly established in the United States by the beginning of the twentieth century, and it was also at about this time that the test began to undergo a series of challenges in the courts. In United States v. Kennerly, 209 F. 119 (1913), Judge Learned Hand criticized the test as being unduly harsh. He gave two reasons for his criticism.

First, the test judged literature in terms of those most open to being corrupted. Since children were the most susceptible individuals, they were used as the basis for the test. Hand stated that the test would "reduce our treatment of sex to the standards of a child's library in the supposed interest of a salacious few...." Hand also criticized the test because it permitted judges to isolate allegedly obscene passages from their setting as a whole. Hand reasoned that obscene material by itself might not be so obscene if it were "honestly relevant to the expansion of innocent ideas...." In other words, a scientific work could be banned as obscene if it so much as contained one instance of obscenity. Judge Hand simply found the test was outdated. The Hicklin test did not "answer to the understanding and morality of the present time...." Despite his objections, however, Judge Hand applied the test because he felt he was required to by precedent; consequently, the test remained an effective force in twentieth century obscenity law.

The second major case invoking the Hicklin test came in 1933 in United States v. One Book Entitled Ulysses, 5 F.Supp. 182 (1933). The Court held James Joyce's Ulysses not obscene. The Court also rejected the Hicklin test and established a new test for determining obscenity. It was held that the first inquiry was whether the material was written with "pornographic intent." If the author's intent was pornographic then the book would be judged obscene. However, if there was no pornographic intent, courts could then look to the work's effect upon the average member of the community. The Court's opinion stated that obscenity decisions should be based upon the work in its entirety, not on the alleged obscene nature of isolated passages of the book. Finally, it was established that if a work which was determined to contain pornographic intent tended to "stir the lustful thoughts," it would be deemed obscene. The second circuit Court of Appeals affirmed the decision. Although the new test was limited to that circuit, it greatly reduced the impact of the Hicklin test and signaled a relaxation of the then existing obscenity standards.

However, some federal courts continued to abide by the Hicklin test as late as the early 1950's. For example, in 1953, a Federal District Court in California applied the Hicklin test to two books by Henry Miller. Viewing only isolated passages of Miller's Tropic of Cancer and Tropic of Capricorn the court held both books to be obscene. The decision was also affirmed by the Ninth Circuit Court of Appeals.

Although the Hicklin test was being eroded by federal courts in New York, it remained a powerful legal force in the state courts. In 1944 Lady Chatterly's Lover by D.H. Lawrence, was held obscene by a New York court in People v. Dial Press, 182 Misc. 416. Several years earlier a Massachusetts bookseller was convicted for selling copies of An American Tragedy by Theodore Dreiser in Commonwealth v. Fried, 271 Mass. 318 (1930). Both state courts relied exclusively on the Hicklin test in making their determinations. State Courts continued to rely on the Hicklin test through the 1950's.

By the 1950's obscenity law in the United States was by no means uniformly applied. A book that would be held obscene by a federal court in California might not be held obscene by a federal court in New York. Furthermore, most state courts would apply a more stringent standard than any of the federal courts. Whether a work was obscene often depended on where the suit was brought. By the 1950's the definition of obscenity was long ripe for adjudication by the United States Supreme Court.

Chapter 2
THE SUPREME COURT SPEAKS – *ROTH v. UNITED STATES*

In addition to establishing a uniform test for obscenity, the Supreme Court was also compelled to determine the constitutional implications of permitting the censoring of obscene material. Specifically, the Supreme Court had yet to determine whether obscene material was an exception to the First Amendment. The First Amendment prohibits Congress from passing any law abridging the freedom of speech or press. Although the Supreme Court seemed to assume in several earlier decisions that obscenity was an exception to the First Amendment, it had never dealt directly with that issue. Finally, in 1957 the Court sought both to define obscenity and to rule on its standing in regard to the First Amendment.

The case was Roth v. United States, 354 U.S. 976 (1957). There, Samuel Roth was convicted for violating Federal Obscenity Statute, 18 U.S.C. 1461 (see Appendix B). Roth was convicted because he sold books and magazines that authorities claimed were obscene. Another case heard along with Roth's was that of Alberts who had been convicted for selling obscene material by a California State

Court. Both Roth and Alberts claimed the materials they were selling were protected under the First Amendment.

The Supreme Court ruled obscene material was not protected by the First Amendment. Relying on the history of obscenity, Justice Brennan, writing for the majority, held that "the unconditional phrasing of the First Amendment was not intended to protect every utterance." According to the Court the First Amendment was by no means absolute; consequently obscenity was not to be within the area of constitutionally protected speech or press.

The Roth Court found that the purpose of the First Amendment would not be served by allowing obscenity constitutional protection. Brennan noted that the protections afforded free speech and press were there to assure "unfettered interchange of ideas for the bringing about of political and social changes desired by the people." The Court found that obscene material possessed little, if any, social value. Furthermore, it was damaging to public morals. Quoting from Chaplinsky v. New Hampshire, 315 U.S. 568 (1942), the Roth Court stated:

> There are certain well-defined and narrowly limited classes of speech, the prevention and punishment of

> which have never been thought to raise any Constitutional problem. These include the lewd and obscene . . . . It has been well observed that such utterances are no essential part of any exposition of ideas, and are of such slight social value as a step to truth that any benefit that may be derived from them is clearly outweighed by the social interest in order and morality. . . .

Having established that obscene material is not protected by the Constitution, the Roth Court found itself faced with another difficult question: how to define obscenity. At the outset, the Court explicitly denounced and rejected the Hicklin test as "unconstitutionally restrictive of the freedoms of speech and press." Instead the Court sought to formulate a less restrictive test which would be more likely to prevent constitutionally protected speech and press from being labeled obscene.

The Court established that obscene material "deals with sex in a manner appealing to the prurient interest." The term "prurient" meant "material having a tendency to excite lustful thoughts." However, the Court made it clear that the showing of sex in art, literature, and scientific works was not itself enough reason to deny material the protections of freedom of speech and press. The Court stated:

> All ideas having even the slightest redeeming social importance -- unorthodox ideas, controversial ideas, even ideas hateful to the prevailing climate of opinion -- have the full protection of the guaranties, unless excludable because they encroach upon the limited area of more important interests. But implicit in the history of the First Amendment is the rejection of obscenity as utterly without redeeming social importance.

In conclusion, the Roth Court established a two-part test for obscenity. The first part asked:

> Whether the average person applying contemporary community standards, the dominant theme of the material taken as a whole appeals to the prurient interest.

The second part of the Roth test asked whether the material in question was "utterly without redeeming social importance." In other words, even if the alleged obscene material appealed to the prurient interest, it would not be obscene if it were shown to possess some redeeming social importance. Applying this test the Court affirmed the convictions of both

Alberts and Roth for selling obscene material.

The dissent, however, pointed out a number of problems with the Roth test. Justice Harlan had three major difficulties with the majority's decision. First, Harlan believed the Court was not specific enough in what it meant by "redeeming social importance." Did the term include only political and social works, or entertainment and artistic works as well? Second, Harlan criticized the Court's ambiguous use of the term "prurient interest." Harlan rightly believed that one person may interpret the term to encompass the slightest sexual desire, while another would interpret it only to encompass extreme perversion. Finally, Harlan did not believe it was the Supreme Court's job to regulate public morals; this job belonged to the states. He noted the dangers of establishing a degree of federal censorship and concluded that such decisions regarding censorship be left up to the states. If the Court were to establish a definition of obscenity, Harlan believed, it should only encompass "hard-core" pornography.

In another dissent, Justices Douglas and Black went even further than Harlan. They believed that obscene material was protected by the First Amendment. They relied on the absolutist phrasing of the

Amendment to reach their decision. Black and Douglas believed the First Amendment protected any "utterance" unless those utterances are "so closely brigaded with illegal action as to be an inseparable part of it." Since obscenity was to be protected by the First Amendment, both Black and Douglas found the federal obscenity statute, under which Roth was convicted, unconstitutional.

Douglas and Black had an interpretation of the First Amendment which differed substantially from that held by the <u>Roth</u> majority. Both justices believed the <u>Roth</u> tests wrongfully punished people for thoughts provoked rather than overt acts. Specifically, the tests convicted those who sold material which only aroused sexual thoughts. Douglas and Black both believed the First Amendment hinged on the free exchange of thoughts, no matter how disagreeable they might be to others. Douglas stated:

> The legality of a publication in this country should never be allowed to turn either on the purity of thought which it instills in the mind of the reader or on the degree to which it offends community conscience. By either test the rule of the censor is exalted and society's values in literary freedom are sacrificed.

Both Black and Douglas concluded that society's interest in unrestricted speech far outweighed the Court's interest in trying to regulate obscene material.

In spite of the several criticisms and potential problems with the Roth opinion, it resolved several questions of obscenity law. First, Roth made it clear that obscene material was not protected by the Constitution. Second, the Court rejected the Hicklin test. From Roth on, allegedly obscene material could not be judged by isolated passages or on its impact upon the most susceptible individuals. The Roth opinion seemed to impose a much more flexible standard. Although Roth had its shortcomings, which will be discussed below, it remains the cornerstone of modern obscenity law.

Chapter 3
THE *ROTH* TEST IS MODIFIED

By the mid 1960's it became clear that Roth had opened a Pandora's Box of problems for American obscenity law. The major problem still lay in the definition of obscenity. In cases involving obscenity, this problem often left the Justices very divided and frequently the Court could not produce a majority. In an effort to improve the situation, the Supreme Court made a number of modifications on the Roth test. They will be discussed in this chapter.

The first major modification on the Roth standard came in 1962, in Manual Enterprises v. Day, 370 U.S. 478. The Postmaster General had prohibited Manual Enterprises from using the mails to transport magazines which were judged to be obscene. The Postmaster reached this decision after finding out the magazines contained pictures of nude male models. A district court agreed with the Postmaster General and found that the materials violated the federal obscenity law.

On appeal, the Supreme Court reversed. However, there was no majority decision. Justice Harlan, joined by Justice Stewart announced the decision of the

Court. In finding the magazines not to be obscene, Harlan held that the "prurient interest" test in Roth was not enough to establish obscenity. Instead, Harlan stated that if material is to be obscene it must also be "patently offensive." In fact, Harlan held, material must be deemed "patently offensive" before it may be subjected to the "prurient interest" test. By "patently offensive" Harlan meant the material must be "so offensive on [its] face as to affront current community standards of decency." As applied to the facts of the case, Justice Harlan did not find the pictures of nude male models "patently offensive." Therefore the Roth test was inapplicable and the pictures could not be held obscene.

Another important aspect of Manual Enterprises was Harlan's treatment of the "redeeming social importance" requirement set forth in Roth. Harlan noted that the magazines in question possessed no scientific, literary, or artistic value. Yet the material was still held not obscene; consequently Harlan established that material need not possess some "social redeeming importance" in order to escape being labeled obscene.

Manual Enterprises is important for two reasons. First, it limited the scope of the Roth test by requiring that material first be shown to be "patently offensive."

Second, it also limited the scope of Roth by establishing that material lacking any "redeeming social importance" may not be obscene. By making these changes Harlan was able to move the Court closer to a definition of obscenity which only encompassed "hard-core" pornography, something he strongly advocated in Roth.

Unfortunately, the Court's problems with obscenity were still growing, and the decision in Manual Enterprises did little to help. No one really knew what was meant by "patently offensive" or for that matter, "prurient interest." People's idea as to what had "redeeming social value" differed from one to the next. The number of obscenity cases on the Court's docket continued to rise.

In 1964, the Supreme Court handed down its decision in Jacobellis v. Ohio, 378 U.S. 184. Jacobellis, who was a manager of a movie theatre, was convicted in Ohio State Court for exhibiting obscene films. Again the issue on appeal to the Supreme Court was whether the material was obscene. Again a divided Court said it was not.

Although Brennan conceded the Roth test was by no means perfect, he emphasized it was the best test the Court could formulate. He stated "we think any substitute [test] would raise equally difficult problems, and we therefor adhere to that standard." Brennan paid specific attention to the "redeeming social importance" criteria:

> We would reiterate, however, our recognition in Roth that obscenity is excluded from the constitutional protection only because it is 'utterly without redeeming social importance,' and that 'the portrayal of sex, e.g., in art, literature, and scientific works, is not itself sufficient reason to deny material the constitutional protection of freedom of speech and press.' . . . .Nor may the constitutional status of the material be made to turn on a 'weighing' of its social importance against its prurient appeal, for a work cannot be proscribed unless it is 'utterly' without social importance.

The Brennan decision also adopted the "patently offensive" requirement set up in Manual Enterprises. Applying this criteria he found the film shown by Jacobellis was not obscene. Justices White, Black and Douglas concurred on grounds similar to those established in the Douglas-Black dissent in Roth. Chief Justice Warren, Justices Clark, and Harlan dissented. All three felt the states should be given more leeway in making obscenity judgments.

Justice Brennan's decision in Jacobellis made one very substantial change in the Roth standard. The "prurient interest" test in Roth was originally to be based on community standards. Brennan, however, asserted that the community standards test referred to a national standard. By adopting a national standard Brennan hoped to establish a uniform definition of obscenity, rather than let each community define obscenity for itself.

The Jacobellis decision did not make the definition of obscenity any clearer. In trying to develop a national standard for obscenity, Brennan failed to realize that different parts of the country might have different attitudes toward, and hence, different definitions of obscenity. Furthermore, the same could be said for his "redeeming social importance" standard. It seemed that the only way one could really determine whether material was obscene was to have the U.S. Supreme Court decide. Justice Stewart seemed to typify the Court's frustration with obscenity when he stated in his Jacobellis dissent:

> I shall not today attempt to define the kinds of material I understand to be embraced within that short-hand definition; and perhaps I could never succeed in intelligibly doing so. But

> I know it when I see it and the motion picture involved in this case is not that.

In 1965, the Court again was faced with another major obscenity case. In Memoirs v. Massachusetts, 383 U.S. 413 , the question before the Court was whether John Cleland's book entitled Memoirs of a Woman of Pleasure was obscene as found by a Massachusetts State Court. Again the Court could reach no consensus, and there was no majority opinion. Justice Brennan joined by Chief Justice Warren and Justice Fortas announced the Court's decision holding the book not obscene.

Taking into account the Court's previous obscenity decisions, Brennan held obscenity could be determined by applying a three part test. First the material must be "patently offensive." Second, the dominant theme of the material must appeal to the "prurient interest." Third, the material must be utterly without redeeming social value.

Applying the test to the book Brennan found it could not satisfy the third requirement, i.e., that the book was not "utterly without redeeming social value." Specifically, Brennan noted that the state court had admittedly found the book to possess literary merit. Furthermore, the state court also found the book to have played a part in the development of the English novel. With these factors in mind, Brennan reasoned the book could not be deemed utterly without redeeming social value and therefore not obscene.

After the Memoirs case, the Roth standard had officially been transformed into a three part test. As evidenced by Memoirs the hardest part of the new test to satisfy was that the material be "utterly without redeeming social value." (Almost anything could be shown to possess some social value.) In a sense, after Memoirs the court had narrowed the constitutional definition of obscenity to include only hard-core pornography. Following 1965, it was very difficult for anything to be held obscene. This practice was not to be changed until 1973.

Chapter 4
APPLYING THE *ROTH* TEST: SOME VARIATIONS

Throughout the sixties the Supreme Court not only modified the Roth test itself, but it also varied the way in which it was applied. For example, in some situations the Court chose not to apply the test at all. In others, application of the test was to be either limited or extended. This chapter will discuss five situations where obscenity tests are not typically applied. The first is that the obscenity exception may not be used to prohibit the dissemination of ideas. The second takes place when obscene material is distributed to "deviant groups." The third occurs when there is evidence of "pandering." The fourth concerns dissemination to minors. The fifth deals with the private use of obscene materials in one's home.

Two years after the Supreme Court handed down its decision in Roth, the Court was faced with a major case concerning the constitutional scope of the Roth standard. In Kingsley Picture Corp. v. Regents, 360 U.S. 684 (1959), New York State denied Kingsley a license to show the film version of Lady Chatterly's Lover because a New York law prohibited the granting of a license to any film which portrayed acts of sexual immorality. The

New York Court of Appeals upheld the denial because it found that three isolated passages of the film which advocated adultery were immoral. Interestingly, the New York Court of Appeals explicitly stated that the film itself was not obscene.

On appeal the Supreme Court reversed the state's decision to deny Kingsley a movie license on the ground that the statute violated the First Amendment. Justice Stewart delivered the opinion of the Court. Stewart explained that immorality is a concept totally different from obscenity or pornography. He found the New York law limited access to materials not because they were obscene, but because of the idea portrayed. In Kingsley, the materials were not obscene and therefore had First Amendment protection. Stewart concluded that a film could not be banned simply because of the idea it conveyed. He stated:

> What New York has done, therefore, is to prevent the exhibition of a motion picture because that picture advocates an idea. . . . Yet the First Amendment's basic guarantee is of freedom to advocate ideas. The State, quite simply, has thus struck at the very heart of constitutionally protected liberty.

This decision points out the crucial principle that the obscenity exception to the First Amendment does not apply to the dissemination of ideas.

The second situation occurs when obscene material is disseminated to a "deviant group." In Mishkin v. New York, 383 U.S. 502 (1966), the Supreme Court held material distributed only to a deviant sexual group could still be held obscene if it appealed to the "prurient interest" of the members of the group. The fact that the material might not appeal to the "prurient interest" of the public as a whole was not dispositive. For example Mishkin involved the dissemination of materials depicting scenes of homosexuality. Such material would not normally appeal to the "prurient interest" of those outside the homosexual community. Nevertheless the Court stated:

> Where the material is designed for and primarily disseminated to a clearly defined deviant sexual group, rather than the public at large, the prurient-appeal requirement of the Roth test is satisfied if the dominant theme of the material taken as a whole appeals to the prurient interest in sex of the members of that group.

In Mishkin the Court made it clear that the scope of the term "obscenity" could vary depending on the group for whom the materials are intended.

The third situation occurs where there is evidence of "pandering." In Ginzberg v. New York, 383 U.S. 463 (1966), the Supreme Court upheld a conviction for mailing obscene materials and related advertising circulars. The decision was based on what the Court termed a "pandering" method of marketing. The Court reached its decision in spite of the fact that the material, by itself, was not obscene. The advertising appeal which focused on perversion was enough to tip the scale in favor of a finding of obscenity. The Ginzberg Court established that "in close cases evidence of pandering may be probative with respect to the nature of the material in question and thus satisfy the Roth test." After Ginzberg it was clear that the scope of obscenity could vary depending on the type of advertising tactics used to market the material.

The fourth situation in which obscenity laws will not normally be applied is when children are invoked. In Ginsberg v. New York, 390 U.S. 629 (1968), the Supreme Court held that a state could bar the distribution of obscene books to children which otherwise were suitable for adults. Ginsberg was convicted of selling pornographic magazines to minors in violation of a New York statute which prohibited the knowing sales to minors under 17 of any picture that depicts nudity, and which:

> (1) appeals to the prurient interest of minors and
> (2) is patently offensive for minors, and
> (3) is utterly without redeeming social importance for minors.

The Supreme Court affirmed Ginsberg's conviction. Justice Brennan, writing for the majority, held that material which may be distributed to adults is "not necessarily constitutionally protected from restriction upon its dissemination to children." The Court provided that the concept of obscenity may vary from one group of people to another. The Court's reason for its decision was clearly stated:

> Because of the State's exigent interest in preventing distribution to children of objectionable material, it can exercise its power to protect the health, safety, welfare and morals of its community by barring the distribution to children of books recognized to be suitable for adults.

The Ginsberg decision established that materials that were not obscene when viewed by adults could be obscene if viewed by children.

The fifth and final situation occurs when obscene materials are used privately. In 1969 the Supreme Court held in the case Stanley v. Georgia, 394 U.S. 557, that the First Amendment prohibited making mere private possession of obscene material a crime. The facts of Stanley are as follows: police entered Stanley's home under a search warrant seeking evidence of gambling activity. Instead, the police found and seized three reels of obscene film. Stanley was subsequently convicted for "knowingly having possession of obscene matter."

The Supreme Court unanimously reversed Stanley's conviction. Justice Marshall, writing for the Court, distinguished Stanley from other obscenity cases because it only induced the private possession of obscene material. All other obscenity cases had involved some public use of such material. Justice Marshall emphasized the importance of one's privacy while in the home. This concept of privacy is strongly enforced by the constitution. Marshall stated:

> If the First Amendment means anything, it means that a State has no business telling a man, sitting alone in his own house, what books he may read or what films he may watch. Our whole constitutional heritage rebels at the thought of

giving government the power to control men's minds.

After Stanley it was clear that any person could possess obscene materials in his home.

Chapter 5
THE 1973 OBSCENITY DECISIONS

As pointed out earlier the obscenity standard set forth in Roth and modified in subsequent cases did not provide an accurate test for determining obscenity. The test called for the application of extremely vague and subjective phrases. As a result, judges and juries were constantly forced to ask themselves a number of difficult questions. For example, what is "patently offensive"; what is "utterly without social redeeming value"; what was "prurient interest."

By the early 1970's, it was clear that the obscenity standard would have to be changed, or at least, more clearly defined. By 1973 a number of new justices had been added to the Supreme Court, including a new Chief Justice - Warren Burger. For the first time since Roth, the Supreme Court was able to put together a solid majority to deal with the obscenity issue. The Burger court made a substantial effort to further define obscenity. The new definition was formulated and applied in a series of Supreme Court decisions handed down in 1973.

Miller v. California

The most famous of the 1973 decisions was Miller v. California, 413 U.S. 15. Miller conducted a mass mailing of brochures which advertised four sex-oriented books. The brochures themselves primarily contained explicit pictures of men and women engaging in several different sexual acts. The new Burger majority voted five to four to uphold Miller's conviction for mailing obscene material.

Writing for the majority, Chief Justice Burger established a new test for obscenity. He wrote:

> [W]e now confine the permissible scope of such regulation [of obscene materials] to works which depict or describe sexual conduct. That conduct must be specifically defined by the applicable state law, as written or authoritatively construed. A state offense must also be limited to works which, taken as a whole, appeal to the prurient interest in sex, which portray sexual conduct in a patently offensive way, and which, taken as a whole, do not have serious literary, artistic, political, or scientific value.

Although the new test may seem similar to the old one, it incorporated some substantial changes. First, and most important, the Miller test did not require that a work be "utterly without redeeming social value" to be obscene. Instead, the Miller test only required that material not have "serious value." In making this change the Miller test made it easier to establish a finding of obscenity. Under the Roth test material could not be held obscene as long as some showing could be made that it possessed some minor degree of redeeming social value. Clearly, the Roth standard had been tightened.

Second, the Miller majority gave examples of what it believed would constitute the term "patently offensive." The opinion stated:

> (a) Patently offensive representations or descriptions of ultimate sexual acts, normal or perverted, actual or simulated. (b) Patently offensive representation or descriptions of masturbation, excretory functions, and lewd exhibition of the genitals.

In further defining the term "patently offensive," the Court made clear to the states exactly what sexual acts were to be deemed obscene, and thus prohibited.

Although the Miller opinion did not specifically address the term "prurient interest," it did refer to the types of material which may be prohibited. The opinion stated:

> Under the holdings announced today, no one will be subject to prosecution for the sale or exposure of obscene materials unless these materials depict or describe patently offensive 'hard-core' sexual conduct specifically defined by the regulating state law, as written or construed.

To this extent the Miller Court was only willing to prohibit "hard-core" pornography. If the prurient interest of someone were aroused by material which was not "hard-core," the material could not be labeled obscene.

Finally, the Miller opinion made it clear that obscenity was not to be judged on a national standard. The Chief Justice found that only on a community-by-community standard could the obscenity tests be effectively applied. Chief Justice Burger believed it would be impossible to set uniform national standards describing precisely what appeals to the "prurient interest" or is "patently offensive." He stated:

> It is neither realistic nor constitutionally sound to read the First Amendment as requiring that the people of Maine or Mississippi accept public depiction of conduct found tolerable in Las Vegas or New York City.

By requiring obscenity to be judged according to the prevailing standard of the community in which the trial takes place, material could be found obscene in one area of the U.S. and not in another.

In dissent, Justice Douglas insisted the new test was unconstitutionally vague. He believed that the Miller test, like the Roth test, did not give the public fair warning as to what material could not be published:

> To send men to jail for violating standards they cannot understand, construe, and apply is a monstrous thing to do in a nation dedicated to fair trials and due process.

Justice Douglas also continued to address his fundamental disagreement with the Court's position on obscenity: that it is not outside the protection of the First Amendment. "The idea that the First Amendment permits Government to ban publications that are 'offensive' to some people puts an ominous gloss on freedom of the press." If Douglas had had his way, no material, no matter how obscene, could be banned.

Although the Miller Court reaffirmed the Roth holding that obscene materials were not protected by the First Amendment, the Court substantially modified the standard for determining what constitutes obscenity. First, only "hard-core" pornography could be prohibited. Second, the material must not possess any "serious value." Third, material was to be judged on a community-by-community basis. Finally, specific guidelines were drawn as to what material can be deemed "patently offensive." The Miller criteria today remains the constitutional test for obscenity. As one will see, all subsequent obscenity cases will be decided in light of Miller.

PARIS ADULT THEATRE v. SLATON

The next case among the 1973 obscenity cases was Paris Adult Theatre v. Slaton, 413 U.S. 49 (1973). Petitioners owned and operated an adult theatre in Georgia. In 1970, a local district attorney filed a complaint alleging that the petitioners were exhibiting two obscene films. The films were entitled "Magic Mirror" and "It All Comes Out in the End." The two films depicted simulated fellatio and group sex intercourse. The door to the theatre read: "Adult Theatre -- you must be 21 and able to prove it. If viewing the nude body offends you, please do not enter." There was no evidence that minors entered the theatre.

Although the trial judge assumed the films were obscene, he dismissed the case because the theatre did not admit minors. On appeal, the Georgia Supreme Court unanimously reversed, holding that such films, because they were obscene, were outside the scope of the First Amendment and therefore should be banned.

On appeal, the U.S. Supreme Court established an important rule in modern obscenity law: that obscene films are not protected from prosecution simply because their exhibition is limited to consenting adults. The Court stated:

> In this case we hold that the states have a legitimate interest in regulating commerce in obscene material and in regulating exhibition of obscene material in places of public accommodation, including so-called "adult" theaters from which minors are excluded.

The Court reasoned that there was a legitimate state interest in safeguarding against crime and the other ill effects that arguably would result from obscenity. The Court agreed that states could determine whether a connection between obscenity and antisocial behavior existed. If so, the state could constitutionally deny adults the right to view obscene material. (This argument will be examined further in the next chapter.)

Justice Brennan, strongly dissented. He adopted some of the points made by Justice Douglas in previous cases. First, the statutes adopted by states to prohibit obscenity were simply too vague. They did not provide adequate notice of what was prohibited. Therefore, Brennan argued, obscenity statutes caused a "chilling effect" upon the First Amendment's freedoms of speech and press. Brennan stated:

> As a result of our failure to define standards with predictable application to any given piece of material, there is no probability of regularity in obscenity decisions by state and lower federal courts. That is not to say that these courts have performed badly in this area or paid insufficient attention to the principles we have established. The problem is, rather, that one cannot say with certainty that material is obscene until at least

five members of this Court, applying inevitably obscure standards, have pronounced it so. The number of obscenity cases on our docket gives ample testimony to the burden that has been placed upon this Court.

Second, Brennan objected to the requirement that material possess no "serious value" before it be held obscene. Brennan stated:

> [The] Court's approach necessarily assumes that some works will be deemed obscene -- even though they clearly have some social value -- because the State was able to prove that the value, measured by some unspecified standard, was not sufficiently "serious" to warrant constitutional protection. That result [is] nothing less than a rejection of the fundamental First Amendment premises and rationale of the Roth opinion and an invitation to widespread suppression of sexually oriented speech.

Brennan held as he did in <u>Roth</u> fifteen years before that to be banned for obscenity, material must be "utterly without redeeming social importance."

He concluded that no precise statute could be "devised to take care of the obscenity problem." No matter what guidelines the Court could draw up, Brennan believed, there would always be a need for judicial judgment. The fact that the Miller majority may have given specific examples of what explicit sexual behavior was obscene was of no matter. He found the Miller test to be inherently similar to the Roth test, and consequently, found no end in sight for the Court's trouble with obscenity.

Finally, Brennan gave what he thought to be the most viable alternative to the Miller test. He said:

> I would hold . . . that at least in the absence of distribution to juveniles or obtrusive exposure to unconsenting adults, the First and Fourteenth Amendments prohibit the state and federal governments from attempting wholly to suppress sexually oriented materials on the basis of their allegedly 'obscene' contents. Nothing in this approach precludes those governments from taking action to serve what may be strong and legitimate interests through regulation of the manner of distribution of sexually oriented material.

By prohibiting obscene material only in the case of unconsenting adults and juveniles, Brennan sought to reduce the obscenity problem to a judicially manageable and constitutionally acceptable level. Brennan believed that if one were to adopt the reasoning set forth by the majority in Paris Adult Theatre (i.e., that obscenity causes antisocial behavior) there would be no limit to a state's power to ban certain books or films.

KAPLAN v. CALIFORNIA

Another of the 1973 cases was Kaplan v. California, 413 U.S. 115. It raised the issue of whether written words in a book could be held obscene just as pictures or movies. The Court held that they could.

Kaplan was a proprietor of an adult bookstore in California. He was later convicted of violating the state's obscenity law. Specifically, an undercover police officer purchased a book from Kaplan entitled 'Suite 69.' After examining the book, a jury convicted Kaplan of selling obscene material. The key factor in the case was that the book was not illustrated.

On appeal, the U.S. Supreme Court affirmed Kaplan's conviction. The Court held that obscene books were not protected by the First Amendment simply because they were not illustrated. Chief Justice Burger, again writing for the majority, noted that books can last for many years and may be passed from one person to another. Burger reasoned it would not be difficult to foresee such books winding up in the hands of youths. Therefore the Court decided California was within its rights to prohibit the sale of such a book.

Interestingly, the Court also re-emphasized the importance of determining obscenity on a community basis. The Court explained that once a jury had found a particular work to be obscene, it would be difficult for an appeals court to overturn such a finding. Whether material is "patently offensive" or appealing to the "prurient interest" are questions of fact. The Court believed that appellate judges should not be allowed to substitute their own judgment for that of the jury. In this respect the Supreme Court was re-affirming its position in Miller that questions of obscenity be decided on a local level.

In its 1973 obscenity decisions, the Court made it easier for states to define obscenity. As long as a jury could find that the alleged obscene material was "patently offensive," appealing to the "prurient interest," and without "serious value" it could be held obscene. States were given a good deal of leeway to define these terms in their own obscenity statutes as long as they were aimed at preventing "hard-core" sexual conducts. Finally, obscenity was to be judged on a community-by-community basis. What was obscene in New Jersey might not be obscene in New York. Although this is an inconsistent application of the First Amendment, the new majority believed that this was the only effective way in which obscenity law could be applied.

The dissents raised several key points. First, the new Miller standard was not much different from the Roth standard. The terms used to define obscenity were still just as vague and subjective. Therefore, citizens would not be given fair notice of what constituted obscenity and the First Amendment rights of many would be violated. Many obscenity cases would continue to make their way up to the Supreme Court. In sum, the obscenity situation would change little from that of before 1973. Second, without a national standard for obscenity, its application would vary from community to community. This standard would inevitably lead to a lack of uniformity in the law which the First Amendment does not tolerate. Finally, there was no concrete evidence that obscene material affected antisocial behavior. The fact that a bare majority of the Court felt that it might was not enough to prohibit it from viewing by consenting adults.

Unfortunately for Justice Brennan and those on the Court who agreed with him, dissents do not make law. The Miller standard today remains the foundation of all decisions regarding obscenity and pornography. Without the background of these earlier cases it would be difficult to understand the later ones, some of which will be discussed in the following chapters.

Chapter 6
THE EFFECT OF PORNOGRAPHY ON ITS VIEWERS

As Justice Douglas repeatedly pointed out in his dissents in the obscenity decisions, the First Amendment is written in absolute terms. It prohibits the creation of any law infringing upon free speech or press. Therefore, Douglas asserted, forms of speech and press could not be banned unless they could be shown to cause immediate illegal action. However, until 1973 the Supreme Court had little, if any, data on the effects of pornography upon those exposed to it. Instead, in 1957 the Roth Court held pornography outside the protection of the First Amendment primarily because it possessed no "redeeming social importance." Since Roth, it has been apparent that a majority of the Supreme Court has found something harmful about the presence of obscene and pornographic material in society. Does the Court believe that those who view obscene material may be driven to illegal action? Or is this theory limited to children?

In 1967, in an effort to determine the actual effects of pornographic material upon those exposed to it, Congress set up the Commission on Obscenity and Pornography. After two years of research and an investment of over two million dollars, the commission reported some of the most thorough results ever achieved.

In a nutshell, the Commission found there was no direct correlation between adults who viewed pornographic material and antisocial conduct. The Commission's findings, while not conclusive, showed that sex offenders were not exposed more to pornography than non-sex offenders. On the contrary, trends pointed out that those who had more exposure to pornographic material led healthier sex lives. As a result, the Commission recommended that society be more open and direct in dealing with sexual matters. The Commission even recommended that state and federal regulations prohibiting the distribution of pornographic material to consenting adults be abolished. More recent studies have reinforced the findings of the Commission. Such studies have suggested that earlier exposure to sexual materials would even lessen the development of antisocial attitudes. The available studies tend to shed doubt on the connection between pornography and antisocial conduct. On the other hand, no evidence has conclusively disproved the connection. Nor does it appear such conclusive findings will be made in the near future.

Basically the same findings have been made with regard to children. Although the alleged effect of pornography on children seems to be the most convincing reason for banning such material, available evidence establishes no direct connection between exposure to pornography and juvenile delinquency or problems in sexual development. Again, while nothing is conclusive, studies on juvenile delinquency have tended to corroborate this position. Two studies conducted as part of the Commission on Obscenity and Pornography found no connection between pornographic material and juvenile delinquency. More recent studies have reinforced these findings and have suggested instead that it is the antisocial activities of one's peer group which more likely lead a youth to antisocial conduct. A youth's underlying social position and personal characteristics are also relevant in determining his tendency to become a juvenile delinquent - not his degree of exposure to pornogrpahy.

Prior to the 1973 decisions the Supreme Court used research on the effect of obscenity and pornography to permit private possession of the material. In Stanley v. Georgia, 394 U.S. 557 (1969), Justice Marshall, writing for a unanimous Court stated:

> There appears to be little empirical basis for that assertion. . . Given the present state of knowledge, the State may no more prohibit mere possession of obscene matter on the ground that it may lead to anti-social conduct than it may prohibit possession of chemistry books on the ground that they may lead to the manufacturer of homemade spirits.

However, by 1973 the new conservative majority on the Court was using the lack of conclusive evidence on the effect of obscenity and pornography to keep such materials prohibited. In its 1973 decision reaffirming obscenity's exemption from First Amendment protection, the Court failed to address the fact that while inconclusive, most research had shown no effect between obscenity and antisocial conduct. Instead, throughout their decisions, the Justices chose to impose their own moral views on the subject. This occurrence has led to the creation of a constitutional policy for which there is no conclusive data available. Moreover, the data that is available seems to support a contrary policy.

The major Supreme Court case which dealt with this issue was the 1973 decision in Paris Adult Theatre. In Paris Adult Theatre, the Court established three major reasons as to why obscene and pornographic material was not protected by the First Amendment. First, despite the absence of conclusive proof on the subject, a state could find that a connection between pornography and antisocial conduct could exist. Second, pornographic material lowers the moral quality of life. Third, if such material were made legal for consenting adults, it would still infringe upon the rights of those who did not wish to view it.

The Court reasoned that just because researchers could not establish a connection between pornography and antisocial conduct, it did not automatically mean that such a connection did not exist. But the Court noted that: "Although there is no conclusive proof of a connection between antisocial behavior and obscene material [a state legislature] could quite reasonably determine that such a connection does or might exist."

The Paris Adult Theatre Court upheld the Georgia statute prohibiting obscenity on the ground that throughout history, legislators had acted on "various unprovable assumptions." The Court reasoned that the mere fact that a law reflected an unprovable assumption about what was good for the people, was not enough reason to find the law unconstitutional. The Court refused to "sit as a 'super legislature' to determine the wisdom, need, and propriety of laws that touch economic problems, business affairs, or social conditions." This aspect of the Paris Adult Theatre decision represented the start of a trend by the new conservative majority to defer to the judgment of state legislatures unless more of a definite constitutional infringement could be established.

Second, although the majority conceded "that there is at least an arguable correlation between obscene material and crime," it found obscenity to be the cause of a more subtle problem: a degraded moral quality of life. The Court stated:

> The sum of experience, including that of the past two decades, affords an ample basis for legislatures to conclude that a sensitive, key relationship of human existence, central to family life, community welfare, and the development of human personality, can be debased and distorted by crass commercial exploitation of sex. Nothing in the

Constitution prohibits a State from reaching such a conclusion and acting on it legislatively simply because there is no conclusive evidence or empirical data.

Clearly, a majority of the Supreme Court believed, and continues to believe, that the presence of pornographic and obscene material degrades the quality of life in the U.S. The new conservative majority also believed that this moral interest on behalf of the states was sufficient to override the First Amendment. The fact that the presence of pornography was not known to cause antisocial conduct or illegal action was irrelevant.

Third, the Court found that even if consenting adults were permitted to purchase obscene and pornographic materials, it would affect those persons who wanted nothing to do with such material. Quoting Professor Alexander Bickel, a constitutional scholar, the Court stated:

> A man may be entitled to read an obscene book in his room, or expose himself indecently there. . . . We should protect his privacy. But if he demands a right to obtain the books and pictures he wants in the market, and to foregather in public places -- discreet, if you will, but accessible to

> all -- with others who share his tastes, then to grant him his right is to affect the world about the rest of us, and to impinge on other privacies. Even supposing that each of us can, if he wishes, effectively avert the eye and stop the ear (which in truth, we cannot), what is commonly read and seen and heard and done intrudes upon us all, want it or not.

For these reasons, the Supreme Court found states could constitutionally prohibit the purchase and dissemination of obscene material. Although no conclusive evidence could be gathered to show the harmful effects of such material, the Court made the moral judgment that states could prohibit it anyway.

If the Supreme Court decided to keep obscene material out of the reach of adults despite no proof of an obscenity-antisocial conduct connection, it is clear children will be treated even more strictly. Although studies have tended to show that children exposed to pornographic material are not directly led to antisocial behavior, states are permitted to prevent children from seeing materials otherwise available to adults. The Supreme Court's rationale for this distinction is similar to that set forth in Paris Adult Theatre v. Slaton. The major case on the subject is still Ginsberg v. New York. In Ginsberg the Court stated:

> [To] be sure, there is no lack of 'studies' which purport to demonstrate that obscenity is or is not 'a basic factor in impairing the ethical and moral development [of] youth and a clear and present danger to the people of the state.' But the growing consensus of commentators is that '[w]hile these studies all agree that a causal link has not been demonstrated, they are equally agreed that a causal link has not been disproved either.'

As in Paris Adult Theatre, the Ginsberg Court makes clear that the fact there is no conclusive proof of one theory, does not necessarily disprove another. Therefore, if a state finds that children should be prohibited from seeing materials otherwise available to adults, then such a finding is constitutionally permissible.

Interestingly, the new Supreme Court majority adopted the reasoning set forth by Justice Harlan fifteen years earlier in his opinion in Roth v. United States:

> It is well known, of course, that the validity of this assumption is a matter of dispute among critics, sociologists,

psychiatrists, and penologists. There is a large school of thought, particularly in the scientific community, which denies any causal connection between the reading of pornography and immorality, crime, or delinquency. Others disagree. Clearly it is not our function to decide this question. That function belongs to the state legislature. Nothing in the Constitution requires California to accept as truth the most advanced and sophisticated psychiatric opinion. It seems to be clear that it is not irrational, in our present state of knowledge, to consider that pornography can induce a type of sexual conduct which a State may deem obnoxious to the moral fabric of society. In fact that very division of opinion on the subject counsels us to respect the choice made by the State.

Chapter 7
CHILD PORNOGRAPHY

Child pornography refers to the harmful use of children as sex objects in the production of films and magazines to be publicly sold. Child pornography developed into a major problem in the late sixties and seventies. The attempt by many states and the Supreme Court to deal with this problem will be discussed in this chapter.

By the mid 1970's child pornography had become a highly organized, multimillion dollar industry. Over 260 different magazines were reported to depict children engaging in explicit sexual conduct. Many magazines depicted children, as young as three, engaging in intercourse, masturbation, rape, and sado-masochism. In an effort to protect children the states took legislative action.

By 1981, Congress and forty-eight states had enacted statutes specifically directed at the production of child pornography. (See Appendix E.) Interestingly, at least half of the statutes did not even require that the materials produced be legally obscene. As long as the material, whether it be books, films, or magazines, contained child pornography, it could be banned. In adopting such broad statutes the states hoped to effectively wipe out the child pornography industry. Additionally, twenty states also prohibited the distribution of material depicting children engaged in sexual conduct without requiring that the material be legally obscene. By also prohibiting the distribution of materials containing child pornography, states further hoped to put a stop to its operation.

The statutes which prohibited material that was not legally obscene presented First Amendment problems. In Roth and Miller, the Supreme Court pointed out that obscene material was not protected by the freedoms of speech and press. Although the Court expressed particular concern for the welfare of minors in the area of obscenity in Ginzberg v. New York, it still required that material be deemed obscene before it could be banned. The First Amendment problems of the child pornography statutes were settled in the recent Supreme Court case of New York v. Ferber, 458 U.S. 747 (1982).

New York was one of the twenty states that prohibited the distribution of material depicting children engaged in sexual conduct without requiring that the materials be obscene. Specifically, the New York statute made it a "D" felony for promoting child pornography. Section 263.05 of the New York Penal Law reads:

> A person is guilty of promoting a sexual performance by a child, when, knowing the character and content thereof, he produces, directs or promotes any performance which includes sexual conduct by a child less than sixteen years of age.

To "promote" is also defined in Section 263.00(5):

> 'Promote' means to procure, manufacture, issue, sell, give, provide, lend, mail, deliver, transfer, transmute, publish, distribute, circulate, disseminate, present, exhibit or advertise, or to offer or agree to do the same.

In 1978, Paul Ferber, who owned a Manhattan bookstore specializing in sexually oriented products, sold two child pornography films to an undercover police officer. The films were devoted mostly to depicting young boys masturbating. Although the jury did not find the films obscene, they convicted Ferber of "promoting a sexual performance by a child." In other words, Ferber broke the law when he sold and distributed child porn material. The fact that the material was not obscene did not bar his conviction.

The New York Court of Appeals reversed the conviction and held that New York's child pornography statute violated the First Amendment. Although the Court recognized the State's interest in protecting children, there was one major reason why the statute could not pass muster under the First Amendment. By not requiring that the films be obscene the statute prohibited too much. The Court found not only did the statute prohibit hard-core pornography, which was permissible, but it also could be read to prohibit the distribution of scientific, educational, and other socially valuable information. As long as the material contained a sexual performance by a minor it could be banned even if its purpose was scientific. The Court of Appeals found the statute to encompass too much and was therefore in violation of the First Amendment.

On appeal however, the U.S. Supreme Court unanimously reversed the New York decision and held the State statute constitutional. The Court held that the states were entitled to "greater leeway" in the regulation of pornography when it involved children. The Court gave several reasons for its decision. First and most important, the Justices took notice of the state's compelling interest in "safeguarding the physical and psychological well-being of a minor." The Court agreed with New York's concern that:

> [T]here has been a proliferation of exploitation of children as subjects in sexual performances. The care of children is a sacred trust and should not be abused by those who seek to profit through a commercial network based upon the exploitation of children. The public policy of the state demands the protection of children from exploitation through sexual performances.

The New York legislature had enacted its statute based on its own findings that the use of children in pornographic films and magazines was harmful to their physical and psychological well-being. The Supreme Court refused to second guess this legislative judgment. The Court concluded that the New York State legislature's judgment, by itself, was enough to make the New York statute constitutional.

However, in footnotes, the Court referred to studies which had been taken to address the effect of child pronography upon its victims. It was found that "the use of children as subjects of pornographic materials is harmful to the physiological, emotional, and mental health of the child.

Specifically it was determined that sexually exploited children are unable to develop healthy relationships in later life. Such children also tended to become sexual abusers as adults. Researchers found children later developed these problems because children who take part in child pornography are often sexually abused by adults involved in its production. Those who are abused tend to become abusers themselves.

Children who are subjects of child pornography are further harmed because their actions are recorded and published. One researcher quoted by the Ferber Court said:

> [P]ornography poses an even greater threat to the child victim than does sexual abuse or prostitution. Because the child's actions are reduced to a recording, the pornography may haunt him in future years, long after the original misdeed took place. A child who has posed for a camera must go through life knowing that the recording is circulating within the mass distribution system for child pornography.

Based on the above findings the Court agreed that a state could easily find that child pornography posed a threat to the mental and physical well being of its subjects.

The Court rejected Ferber's contention that only materials found obscene under the Miller test could be prohibited. The Court held "while some states may find that (the Miller test) properly accommodates its interests, it does not follow that the First Amendment prohibits states from going further." In other words, when the welfare of children was at stake, the Court held that states could go beyond the limits set forth in Miller without violating the First Amendment. The Court stated:

> [T]he question under the Miller test of whether a work, taken as a whole, appeals to the prurient interest of the average person bears no connection to the issue of whether a child has been physically or psychologically harmed in the production of the work. Similarly, a sexually explicit depiction need not be 'patently offensive' in order to have required the sexual exploitation of a child for its production. In addition, a work which, taken on the whole, contains serious literary, artistic, political, or scientific value may nevertheless embody the hardest core of child

pornography. It is irrelevant to the child who has been abused whether or not the material. . . has a literary, artistic, political or social value. We therefore cannot conclude that the Miller standard is a satisfactory solution to the child pornography problem.

The Court also found that states not only had a valid interest in preventing the production of child porn materials, but also in preventing their distribution. Since child pornography was extremely difficult to stop at its source, i.e., its production, states would be permitted to stop it from reaching its market. For this reason, a law prohibiting the distribution of child porn materials was wholly justified.

With these factors in mind, the Ferber Court concluded New York was justified in prohibiting the production and distribution of child porn materials. The fact that the statute did not require material to be obscene did not violate the First Amendment.

THE NEW STANDARD FOR CHILD PORNOGRAPHY

Although the Court retained the Miller standard for cases not involving children, it failed to adopt a specific test for child pornography. The test the Court finally came up with is as follows:

A trier of fact need not find that the material appeals to the prurient interest of the average person; it is not required that sexual conduct portrayed be done so in a patently offensive manner; and the material at issue need not be considered as a whole.

The above test, if it is a test, is nothing more than a negative application of the Miller test. It really tells the states nothing on how to formulate their child pornography laws. As a result, Ferber gives the states great latitude in formulating their own tests for child pornography. The Court's statement that material need not be evaluated "as a whole" allows the material to be judged on the basis of "isolated passages." Since there is no requirement that the material be without "serious value," it would seem this part of the Miller test need not be satisfied to show child pornography. The Ferber test gives states the power to prohibit any material containing even the slightest amount of child sex. This test may be construed to include both scientific and artistic material as well.

In Ginsberg v. New York in 1968 the Supreme Court established its concern for the protection of children in the area of obscenity. Ferber has clearly re-affirmed that concern by removing child pornography from the scope of the First Amendment whether or not it is obscene. The Court's method for doing so is to give the states the discretion to determine for themselves what should be banned.

Chapter 8
PORNOGRAPHY AND THE BROADCAST MEDIA

Earlier chapters have concentrated on pornography in printed works. This chapter will focus on pornography and radio and television. The Miller test for obscene material applies to radio and television just as it applies to printed works. Any radio or television broadcast which satisfies the three elements of the test may be banned. However, because radio and television have accumulated such large audiences over the years, and are so easily accessible to children, Congress and the Supreme Court have regulated the broadcast industry more strictly. Today the law requires both radio and television to maintain a much higher level of decency than that of printed works.

In order to understand why the communications industry is regulated, one must briefly look to its history. Before 1927 the allocation of broadcast frequencies was left entirely to the private sector. Since there were a limited number of frequencies for a virtually unlimited number of broadcasters, the result was mass confusion. There were simply too many voices competing to be heard and not enough frequencies to accommodate them.

Congress thus enacted the Radio Act of 1927, which set up the Federal Radio Commission to allocate frequencies. The Radio Act gave birth to the Communications Act of 1934 which governs telecommunications today (47 U.S.C. §151-609). The purpose of the Act remains to regulate telecommunications in the United States. The administrative body created by Congress to enforce the Act is the Federal Communications Commission (FCC). The FCC is composed of seven members appointed by the President for seven year terms. Under the provisions of the Act the FCC is granted power both to supervise rates and services, and to regulate broadcast licenses.

Although Congress, by necessity, is permitted to regulate broadcasters, this power may not infringe upon First Amendment rights. The Supreme Court pointed out in Red Lion Broadcasting Co. v. FCC, 395 U.S. 367 (1968), that: "the people as a whole retain their interest in free speech by radio and their collective right to have the medium function consistently with the ends and purposes of the First Amendment." The battle to keep pornography off the airwaves pits the First Amendment against the power of Congress to regulate under the Act.

The federal power to regulate the program content of radio and television resides in three conflicting statutes. First, the Communications Act empowers the FCC to regulate broadcasters in the "public interest." Section 303 of the Act empowers the FCC to regulate the communications industry to serve the "public convenience, interest, or necessity." Those radio and television broadcasters who do not serve the "public interest" may have their licenses to operate suspended or revoked by the FCC.

The second is a criminal statute which prohibits the broadcast of indecent or obscene language. Section 1464 of the U.S. Criminal Code reads:

> Whoever utters any obscene, indecent or profane language by means of radio communications shall be fined not more than $10,000 or imprisoned for not more than two years or both.

Finally, the FCC is prohibited by the Communications Act from ever exercising censorship over broadcasters. Section 326 of the Act reads:

> Nothing in this chapter shall be understood or construed to give the Commission the power of censorship over the radio communications or

> signals transmitted by any radio station, and no regulation or condition shall be promulgated or fixed by the Commission which shall interfere with the right of free speech by means of radio communication.

The above three statutes certainly conflict with one another. On the one hand material which does not serve the public interest may not be broadcast. Yet on the other hand this would seem to be censorship that would violate freedom of speech. Furthermore, Section 1464 prohibits the broadcast of indecent and obscene speech. This provision would also seem to violate a broadcaster's freedom of speech and amount to censorship. It would also appear that section 1464 is in conflict with the Miller decision which requires that only material which is judged obscene may be prohibited. Those who wish to keep pornography off the airwaves claim that pornography is both indecent and not in the public interest. Those who wish to permit the broadcast of pornography claim that to do otherwise would amount to censorship in violation of the First Amendment. The questions raised by the conflicting sections were partially answered several years ago in a famous Supreme Court decision.

FCC v. PACIFICA, 438 U.S. 776 (1978)

In 1978 George Carlin, a famous comedian, recorded a twelve minute monologue entitled "filthy words" before a live audience in California. In his performance Carlin repeatedly used words of a profane and vulgar character. Several weeks later a New York radio station owned by the Pacifica Corporation broadcast the performance. A man who heard the broadcast while driving with his son complained to the Federal Communications Commission.

Although the FCC found the monologue "patently offensive" it did not find it obscene. Nevertheless, the FCC issued a declaratory order ruling that such language could be banned from the airwaves. The FCC advanced two reasons for its decision. First, Section 1464 required the Commission to prohibit the broadcast of indecent language. Second, such language was not in the "public interest" and could therefore be prohibited. The FCC also set forth several other policy reasons for its determination, which were:

(1) children have access to radios and in many cases are unsupervised by parents;

(2) radio receivers are in the home, a place where people's privacy interest is entitled to extra deference;

(3) unconsenting adults may tune in a station without any warning that offensive language is being or will be broadcast; and

(4) there is a scarcity of spectrum space, the use of which the government must therefore license in the public interest.

The Pacifica Foundation appealed the Commission's decision to the United States Court of Appeals for the District of Columbia. There, Pacifica argued that the Commission's ruling amounted to censorship and violated the station's freedom of speech. The Court of Appeals agreed with Pacifica and reversed the FCC's decision.

On appeal, the United States Supreme Court, in a narrow five to four decision, reversed. Justice Stevens, writing for the majority gave two major reasons why the decision of the Commission was proper. First, he found that broadcasting has a pervasive presence in American society, and therefore required more stringent regulation than printed works. Second, the broadcast media has a unique accessibility to children. For these reasons the Court found justification for permitting a different level of First Amendment protection for broadcasters, as opposed to printers.

The Pacifica majority found the broadcast of "indecent" speech to be unprotected by the First Amendment because of the large audience reached. Unlike a book or magazine, which must be deliberately purchased, the Court pointed out that broadcasting comes directly into the home with or without invitation.

> Patently offensive, indecent material presented over the airways confronts the citizen not only in public but in the privacy of the home, where the individual's right to be let alone plainly outweighs the First Amendment rights of an intruder.

Pacifica argued that if a listener found a program indecent or offensive he could simply turn the channel or turn the radio off.

In response to this argument the Court replied:

> To say that one may avoid further offense by turning off the radio when he hears indecent language is like saying that the remedy for an assault is to run away after the first blow.

The Court also noted that a prior warning given by the broadcaster notifying listeners that some material might be offensive would not necessarily prevent the listener from hearing such a program.

The decision also ruled that the broadcast of "indecent" speech is unprotected by the First Amendment because of its accessibility to children. Citing the Ginsberg case the Court reasserted the government's interest in safeguarding the well-being of its young. The opinion made it clear that even a child too young to read would have had access to Carlin's monologue. The Court also took note of the authority of parents in their homes to bring children up the way they deem proper. In this respect, it was found that "indecent" broadcasting interfered with that parental right.

Defining Indecency

Having held indecent speech outside the protection of the First Amendment when it is publicly broadcast, the Court went on to define what is meant by the term "indecent." The Pacifica decision defined "indecent" as something that does not conform to "accepted standards of morality." The Court determined that "prurient appeal" which is an element of obscenity, is not an element of indecency.

In other words, indecent speech need not arouse sexual thoughts. Instead the Pacifica majority referred to Carlin's monologue as "patently offensive," "vulgar," "offensive," and "shocking." If part of a radio or television program is found to be patently offensive, vulgar, or shocking it might be labeled indecent and banned.

Dissent

In dissent, Justice Brennan claimed the majority's decision violated the First Amendment rights of both the broadcast media and the people who wanted to hear such programs. Brennan pointed out that the listener himself decides whether or not to invite the broadcast into his home. In short, if the listener does not like what he hears, he may simply turn off the radio. Brennan stated:

> [W]hatever the minimal discomfort suffered by a listener who inadvertently tunes into a program he finds offensive during the brief interval before he can simply extend his arm and switch stations or flick the 'off' button, it is surely worth the candle to preserve the broacaster's right to send, and the right of those interested to receive, a message entitled to full First Amendment protection.

According to Brennan, the majority holding could lead to unlimited censorship of protected speech. This included political and artistic works. Brennan asserted that the Court's decision could:

> [J]ustify the banning from radio of a myriad of literary works, novels, poems, and plays by the likes of Shakespeare, Joyce, Hemingway, Ben Jonson, Henry Fielding, Robert Burns, and Chaucer; they could support the suppression of a good deal of political speech, such as the Nixon tapes; and they could even provide the basis for imposing sanctions for the broadcast of certain portions of the Bible.

Brennan, along with the other three dissenters, made it clear that the majority's decision could give the FCC an unwarranted degree of censorship over broadcasters.

Implications of the Pacifica Decision

The Pacifica decision upholds the FCC's authority to prohibit the broadcast of indecent speech under section 1464. However, unlike obscenity, indecent speech is still afforded some constitutional protection. Indecent speech printed in a book, for example, would still be protected. Quoting from another case, the

Pacifica Court used the example: "[W]hile a nudist magazine may be within the protection of the First Amendment. . . the televising of nudes might well raise a serious question of programming contrary to 18 U.S.C. §1464." The Court's reasons for this distinction is the large audience reached by broadcasters, and the accessibility of the media to children.

Pacifica Corporation claimed that "indecent" is synonymous with "obscene" or "hard-core" pornography. Otherwise, Pacifica alleged, the Government would be entitled to censor whatever it did not feel was morally acceptable. However, the Supreme Court refuted this argument by pointing out that under Pacifica's rationale, only obscene or hard-core pornographic material could be prohibited. Such a standard would allow broadcasters virtually unlimited discretion as to what should be broadcast. The Court was not willing to let public broadcasters go this far; consequently the Pacifica decision restricts the First Amendment rights of broadcasters who wish to transmit non-obscene material.

Finally, the Pacifica decision emphasized the narrowness of its holding, and set forth criteria for the prohibition of offensive broadcasts in the future. The Court noted that its decision only dealt with the FCC's authority to prohibit the broadcast of the Carlin monologue. By requiring that its decision be narrowly construed the Court may have lessened the chance of its decision being extended to cover other forms of media such as cable television. The Court also made it clear that many factors were to be used in determining whether a particular broadcast could be prohibited in the future. The Court said:

> [C]onsideration of a host of variables (is required): The time of day..., the content of the program in which the language is used ... and differences between radio, television and perhaps closed-circuit transmission....

By requiring the FCC to look not only at the content of a broadcast, but also at the context in which the broadcast was made, the Pacifica majority applied what is known as a nuisance law rationale. In this situation, nuisance law concerns the channeling of offensive broadcasts rather than prohibiting them. For example, under a nuisance law rationale Carlin's monologue might not have been prohibited had it been broadcast late at night instead of in the afternoon when children might be listening. In establishing a nuisance law rationale to deal with offensive broadcasts the Court is interested more in channeling an offensive broadcast than simply censoring it. The Court's reasoning still would permit the broadcast of some offensive material while at the same time satisfy its major concern, i.e. that of preventing the broadcast from reaching children.

Despite words of limitation however, the Pacifica decision presents problems for other branches of the media. It is possible that one day the Pacifica decision could be extended to prevent the publication of indecent material in newspapers, magazines, and books. These printed works pervade American society, and to a lesser extent, are also available to minors. The same can be said for motion pictures. Today, the most vulnerable among the media from the implications of Pacifica is cable television.

Chapter 9
CABLE TELEVISION AND PORNOGRAPHY

The issue of the FCC's ability to extend the Pacifica decision to encompass cable television is of major concern to cable television operators and viewers. In light of the large volume of pornographic programs on cable television, it is possible that the Pacifica decision could be broadened to prevent "indecent" broadcasts on cable as well. However, the differences between cable television and broadcast television are so substantial, it seems such an extension of Pacifica would be highly unlikely and damaging to the First Amendment. As of now, with regard to the program content, cable television remains a relatively unregulated part of our telecommunications industry.

Today one can argue that cable television pervades American life to an extent almost equal to that of broadcast television. Over twenty million American homes subscribe to cable television Studies show the number of subscribers increases by over 200,000 a month. It is estimated that by 1985 forty percent of American homes will receive cable television. The predictions for the close of the decade are much higher.

As cable television expands so does the number of pornographic programs it televises. Today, there are at least six cable networks devoted exclusively to pornography. Playboy has its own channel and Penthouse is about to start its own as well. In addition, sex shows like "Midnight Blue" continue to bring graphic nudity into thousands of homes. There is little disagreement that the number of such programs is rapidly increasing.

With the increase of pornographic programs there has also been a corresponding increase in the number of viewer complaints to the FCC. Each year the FCC receives thousands of complaints from viewers upset or offended by certain cable programs. Although a number of solutions have been proposed to regulate the cable industry, nothing has definitely been adopted. Congress, the courts, and the FCC continue to look for a way to control pornography on cable television that is consistent with the demands of the First Amendment. The difficulty in finding a way to regulate cable television, as opposed to broadcast television, lies in its unique nature of operation.

At present, cable television operates differently from broadcast television in three major aspects. First, unlike broadcast television, whch sends over-the-air signals, cable television operates by transmitting programs to subscribers through wires or cables. It is not a public broadcast. In order to receive cable television people must deliberately purchase access to it. Cable programs do not come into the home without invitation the way broadcast television programs do. Furthermore, if the subscriber is offended by cable television he may simply cancel his subscription. Broadcast television on the other hand, requires no subscription. Therefore, if the user of broadcast television is offended by a program he may only complain to the FCC, network or sponsor. Since cable television is not a public transmission, it need not be regulated to the extent of public broadcast television. Therefore, the Pacifica holding would seem not to be applicable.

Second, cable television, unlike broadcast television, has an almost unlimited number of channels. Broadcast television is strictly limited in channel space and must therefore appeal to the greatest number of viewers for revenues. As a result, broadcast television must also strive to offend the least number of viewers. For this reason broadcast television has been accused of programming which is often bland and unprovocative. Cable television, on the other hand, because of its broad ranges of channels, appeals generally to a more specialized viewer. To limit the content and scope of cable programming through regulation would deprive cable television of its special wide-range appeal. Such limitations might conceivably turn cable television into a bland and unprovocative medium of communication like broadcast television.

Third, it should be pointed out that cable companies would provide subscribers with "lockboxes" to prevent viewing of programs by children. A parent not wishing his or her child to view a particular program may simply "lock" the cable box for the duration of the program. Broadcast television does not provide such a service. A problem with "lockboxes" is that many cable companies do not provide them. However, some states have taken legislative action. New York, for example, requires that cable companies sell "lockboxes" on request.

Despite the differences between cable and broadcast television there are a number of similarities which would seem to favor extending the Pacifica holding to cover cable. First, like broadcast television, cable pervades American society whether or not it is publicly or privately transmitted. The Pacifica Court found this factor most persuasive in its decision to keep indecent material off the air. Second, both broadcast and cable television come into the home. As the Supreme Court noted in Pacifica, this factor cuts in favor of limiting First Amendment protection. Third, since cable television comes into the home it may be accessible to children. The Pacifica Court also established this factor as one of its major concerns. Fourth, unlike radio, cable television is a visual depiction which would have much more of an effect upon a viewer. If the Pacifica Court prohibited indecent broadcasting on radio, it is logical to assume the Court could extend its holding to cable television.

Indeed, relying on these factors a number of states and municipalities have enacted or introduced legislation to prohibit cable pornography. For example, in 1981 the State of Utah enacted a statute prohibiting the distribution by wire or cable of "any pornographic or indecent material to its subscribers." (See Appendix G.) The statute defined indecent material as follows:

(1) (a) Human genitals in a state of sexual stimulation or arousal;
(b) Acts of human masturbation, sexual intercourse, or sodomy; or
(c) Fondling or other erotic touching of human genitals, pubic region, buttock, or female breast.

(2) (a) Less than completely and opaquely covered:
(i) Human genitals;
(ii) Pubic regions;
(iii) Buttock; and
(iv) Female breast below a point immediately above the top of the areola; and
(b) Human male genitals in a discernibly turgid state, even if completely and opaquely covered.

The Utah Statute was struck down in 1982 by a Federal District Court for violating the First Amendment. In the case Home Box Office v. Wilkinson, 531 F.Supp. 936 (D. Utah 1982), the Court found the Utah statute in conflict with the Supreme Court's decision in Miller v. California. The decision held that the Miller case establishes that states may only proscribe that material which is obscene. The Utah Statute did not comply with the Miller standard because it prohibited visual depictions which might not necessarily be obscene. Jenkins noted that under the Utah law, movies such as The Godfather, Being There, Kramer vs. Kramer, and Coal Miner's Daughter could be prohibited. The Court not only found the term "indecent" overbroad, it also found there was a less burdensome alternative to prohibiting indecent programs. Judge Jenkins wrote:

Merely calling something 'indecent' doesn't necessarily make it so. At least under some definitions, a high percentage of what we see on television, I think, could very well b~ brought under the umbrella of indecency. I think the appeal to violence is indecent. I think the appeal to the lowest level of the intellect is indecent. I think the appeal to instant gratification is indecent. I think appealing to the worst in all of us is indecent. Those who do ought to be ashamed of themselves. But that does not mean that what they do is proscribed.

We put up with it. What we do if we have occasion to be offended by something in a program is we get up and we turn it off. We do something else. We read a book. We refuse to purchase the sponsor's product. And if we're concerned parents and we're not overjoyed by the violence and stupidity of 'The Dukes of Hazzard', we turn it off and direct our children to something else.

That's one of the nice things about TV -- not just cable TV, but also with the regular broadcast channels that are allocated, licensed and regulated by the government. There is no law that says you have to watch. There is no law that says that you have to purchase a television set. There is no law that says you have to subscribe to a cable TV service any more that you have to subscribe to The Salt Lake Tribune. One of the greatest virtues of our system, I think, is freedom to choose.

Judge Jenkins also rejected the state's argument that the statute was a necessary means to protect the welfare of its children. Citing Supreme Court decisions, Jenkins found that minors are entitled to First Amendment rights. Consequently, only in narrow and well-defined circumstances could a state ban such programs. Since the Utah statute did not refer to children, it was overbroad in regard to adults.

In a Florida case involving similar facts, another federal judge agreed with Judge Jenkins and struck down a Miami City ordinance prohibiting the use of indecent material on cable T.V. (See Cruz v. Ferre, 571 F.Supp. 125 (1983).) Judge Hoeveler outlined the substantial differences between cable television and broadcast television to conclude that the Pacifica decision was inapplicable to cable television Specifically, Hoeveler emphasized the use of "lockboxes" to prevent children from viewing offensive programs:

To protect children or other immature viewers from unsuitable programming, subscribers need only use a free 'lockbox' or 'parental key' available from Cable Vision. This opportunity to completely avoid the potential harm to minor or immature viewers sounds the death-knell of Pacifica's applicability in the cable television context.

In light of these two decisions it seems that only material which can be found legally obscene under the Miller standard may be proscribed on cable television. Nevertheless, states, municipalities, and various organizations continue to devise new ways in which to keep pornography off cable television. (For examples, see Appendix G.) As these lower court decisions involving these laws make their way up to the Supreme Court, the issue of indecency on cable television will be addressed. However, until the Supreme Court speaks, it seems the Pacifica decision will not be broadened to cable television and cable operators will remain free to televise as much non-obscene material as they wish.

Chapter 10
PORNOGRAPHY AND MOTION PICTURES

Although motion pictures were once strictly regulated by states, they are only loosely regulated today; and consequently motion pictures may contain a good deal of pornography. The motion picture industry has remained relatively free from government regulation for two reasons. First, the Supreme Court has held that movies are protected by the First Amendment. Second, in 1968 the industry began regulating itself with its own rating system. Although the rating system is not a constitutional or legal standard, it has proven successful in limiting younger people's access to pornographic movies. This chapter will briefly give an overview of the history of motion pictures and pornography. It will also discuss the formation and operation of the motion picture ratings system.

As far back as 1915 the Supreme Court held that states could censor motion pictures. In the case of Mutual Film Corp. v. Industrial Commission, 236 U.S. 230 (1915), the Court found that movies were not protected speech under the First Amendment. Instead, the Court referred to them as "business pure and simple." Therefore, states were permitted to regulate the movie industry like any other business.

Throughout the early part of this century states soon took advantage of their power to censor motion pictures which were "undesirable" or "immoral." Many states quickly enacted censorship statutes and as a result the motion picture industry was extremely restricted in what it could produce. (See Appendix F for a list of films banned in the early part of this century.) In response to this state action, the Motion Picture Producers and Distributors Association created its own guidelines to regulate movie content. The guidelines, which were very strict, were called the Motion Picture Production Code of 1930. The code established the type of language and visual effects which could not be used. For example, religion could not be demeaned and obscene speech was prohibited. Evil, sin, and crime could not be justified. In effect, the code amounted to the industry's censorship of itself.

The Supreme Court changed its view on motion pictures in 1952 in the landmark decision Burstyn v. Wilson, 343 U.S. 495. At issue in Burstyn was a film by Federico Fellini entitled The Miracle. The film involved a drunken woman who was seduced by a stranger whom she thinks is Saint Joseph. The woman then becomes pregnant and believes it is the result of immaculate conception. After granting the movie a license, the New York State Education Department received much criticism from various Catholic organizations, which called the film "sacriligious." Due to this pressure, the Education Department subsequently rescinded the film's license. The New York Court of Appeals upheld the Department's decision. Joseph Burstyn, the film's distributor, appealed the decision to the U.S. Supreme Court.

The Supreme Court unanimously reversed the state's decision and for the first time held that motion pictures are a "significant medium for the communication of ideas." Since one of the primary purposes of the First Amendment was to protect the free exchange of ideas, the Court held stated motion pictures were entitled to First Amendment protection. The Court held that movie censors could no longer be vested with unlimited censoring powers. To do so would create an unconstitutional prior restraint of protected speech. The fact that a film was sacriligious was not enough to override the First Amendment.

Shortly after Burstyn the Supreme Court reversed five other state court decisions that upheld the censoring of various films. The banning of the movie La Ronde for being "immoral" was reversed. The banning of the movie M for being uneducational was reversed.

The banning of the movie Pinky for not being in the "public interest" was reversed. The banning of The Moon is Blue for being "corrupt" was reversed. Finally, the banning of the movie Native Son for being "conducive to crime" was also reversed.

By the late 1950's the Supreme Court decisions, taken as a whole, indicated that a movie could be banned only if it was obscene or sexually immoral. In 1957, the Supreme Court established that material found legally obscene could be prohibited. (See discussion of Roth, in Chapter 2.) However, the Court reinforced its position that only obscene material could be banned when it decided the case Kingsley Pictures v. Regents, 360 U.S. 684 (1959). In Kingsley, the Court determined that no movie may be banned because it advocates an immoral idea. (See Chapter 4.) After Roth and Kingsley, movie censors could prohibit only obscene films.

Although the Supreme Court worked to free the motion picture industry from state regulation, the Court would not permit films the same First Amendment rights as those granted to literary works. In Times Film Corp. v. Chicago, 365 U.S. 43 (1961), the Court held constitutional a

Chicago ordinance requiring submission of motion pictures to a censorship board prior to their exhibition. Upon finding the film not obscene, the board would issue the film a permit. The ordinance provided that films could not be shown in Chicago without a permit. Times Film Corporation claimed the ordinance was an unconstitutional prior restraint of free speech and refused to submit the film Don Juan. Thereafter, the Chicago Censorship Board refused to issue a permit and the Times Film Corporation went to court.

On finding that films are a different form of expression and therefore entitled to less First Amendment protection, the Supreme Court upheld the Chicago law. Noting that freedom of speech is not absolute the Court stated: "It does not follow that the Constitution requires absolute freedom to exhibit every motion picture of every kind at all times and places." It is interesting to point out that in a previous case the Court expressly held that books could not be pre-screened before publication. Such action would violate the First Amendment. See Bantam Books v. Sullivan, 372 U.S. 58 (1963). Although the Supreme Court established in Times Film Corp. that movies were to be treated differently under the First Amendment, the Court did not see why. Perhaps it is because movies are usual depictions whch have a greater impact on people than literary works. Nevertheless, today states still possess the right to have motion pictures submitted prior to their exhibition.

In an effort to limit state power to pre-screen films the Supreme Court handed down its famous decision, Freedman v. Maryland, 380 U.S. 51. Freedman exhibited the film Revenge at Daybreak without first submitting it to the Maryland Motion Picture Censorship Board. At the time Maryland law required films receive a license from the board prior to exhibition. The statute prohibited exhibition of any disapproved film unless or until the exhibitor could undertake a time-consuming appeal to the Maryland courts. Only if the courts overturned the board's decision could the film be shown. Freedman refused to submit the film because he believed the statute an unconstitutional prior restraint on protected expression. Although the censor board conceded the film was not obscene, Freedman was nevertheless convicted for violating the statute. Maryland's highest court affirmed his conviction and Freedman appealed to the Supreme Court.

The Supreme Court reversed Freedman's conviction. The Court found the statute under which Freedman was convicted was overly burdensome. Under the terms of the law, only if Freedman could get a court to overturn the board's decision would he be able to exhibit his film. This process could take months or years. In the interim the public would be denied access to what might be protected speech. The Court stated:

> [A] State is not free to adopt whatever procedures it pleases for dealing with obscenity. . . without regard to the possible consequences for constitutionally protected speech.

In order to ensure that state laws requiring submission of motion pictures prior to exhibition are constitutional, the Court established a three-part test:

> (a) the burden of proving that the motion picture is obscene must rest on the censor;
>
> (b) the exhibitor must be assured that the censor will either allow exhibition or go to court to restrain exhibition within a specified brief period of time and that any interim restraint will be limited to preservation of the status quo; and
>
> (c) there must be provision for a prompt final judicial decision.

The Freedman Court established these three safeguards as the minimum requirements for state pre-screening legislation. Any state law aimed at pornographic movies must comply with the Freedman test. Otherwise it will be held an unconstitutional prior restraint.

The Ratings System

In 1968 the Supreme Court in Ginsberg v. New York permitted states to redefine obscenity where material was to be viewed by children (see Chapter 4). As a result, states could classify films as suitable or unsuitable for minors. The Ginsberg decision again invited states to regulate the motion picture industry. In the late sixties and seventies there were many nonobscene films which might not be considered "suitable" for minors. Indeed, both federal and state legislation was being introduced to keep minors away from offensive but not obscene films. To stem the tide of such regulation, the Motion Picture Association of America (MPAA) abandoned the outdated Motion Picture Protection Code and adopted its own set of ratings.

On November 1, 1968, the voluntary film rating system of the motion picture industry went into effect. The system then developed is essentially the same as that used today, which has four categories:

G - general audiences, all ages admitted
PG - parental guidance suggested
R - restricted, those under 17 must be accompanied by an adult
X - no one under 17 admitted

There are three major participants in the ratings system: The Motion Picture Association of America (MPAA), an association of 80 television and motion picture organizations; the National Association of Theatre Owners (NATO) which enforces the ratings at the theatre; and International Film Importers and Distributors of America (IFIDA).

The ratings system was a totally new concept. Film producers were no longer bound by the content regulations of the old code. Instead the ratings system enabled them to make movies however they wished. Once made, a movie would then be rated for parents who could then make an informed decision on whether their children should attend. Jack Valenti, President of the MPAA, wrote:

> Under the rating program, the filmmaker became free to tell his story in his way without anyone thwarting

him. The price he would pay for that freedom would be the possible restriction on viewing by children. I held the view that freedom of the screen was not defined by whether children must see everything a filmmaker conceived.

Ratings are arrived at by a Rating Board located in Hollywood. The board is composed of seven members, each of whom need have no specific qualifications. The job of a board member is simply to put himself or herself in the shoes of a parent trying to determine whether the movie is suitable for his or her children. Most films are voluntarily submitted to the board for a rating. The board views each film and after group discussion, votes on the rating. The rating is decided by a majority vote and is based on four factors: language, sex, violence, and theme. A "G" rating means a film contains nothing in these four factors which would, in the opinion of the rating board, be offensive to younger children viewing the film. A "PG" rating means some material may not be suitable for children. Such films may contain profanity, brief nudity and minor violence. However, "PG" movies may not contain anything beyond these. An "R" rating tells parents that a film may contain hard violence, sex and lovemaking, and rough language. In many aspects it is an adult film. Finally, an "X" rating means a film is for adults. In further defining the "X" rating, Jack Valenti stated:

> This is patently an adult film and no children are allowed to attend. It should be noted, however, that X does not necessarily mean obscene or pornographic in terms of sex or violence. Serious films by lauded and skilled filmmakers may be rated X. The Rating Board does not attempt to mark films as obscene or pornographic; that is for the courts to decide legally. The reason for not admitting children to X-rated films can relate to the accumulation of brutal or sexually connected language, or of explicit sex or excessive and sadistic violence.

It should be noted that most producers of pornographic film do not submit their movies to the rating board. Instead they simply give themselves an "X" rating. Only if a film is found legally obscene can it be banned. (For a listing of movies found obscene and prohibited, see Appendix F.) Finally, the decision of the rating board may be appealed to the Ratings Appeal Board, which consists of 24 members of various movie industry organizations. The producer of a film also may edit a film in an effort to obtain a less severe rating.

Although it is well established that ratings may not be used as a constitutional standard, it has worked to help parents to form the moviegoing habits of their children. Because of the system only those 17 years old and over may view pornographic films in movie theatres. The system is far from perfect. But up until now it has adequately served to replace most state regulation.

Chapter 11
ELIMINATING PORNOGRAPHY THROUGH THE USE OF ZONING ORDINANCES

After the Miller decision, municipalities felt helpless to prohibit the establishment of adult bookstores, movie theatres and cabarets unless such centers could first be judged obscene. As recent case law has shown, finding a particular book, movie or performance obscene is not an easy task. For example, the film Caligula, an explicitly violent and pornographic X-rated movie about a mad Roman emperor, was deemed not obscene. Courts determined that although the film both appealed to prurient interest and was patently offensive, it did possess some political value. Supporters of Caligula established that a political theme running throughout the movie was that "absolute power corrupts absolutely." The courts agreed and held that Caligula was not obscene.

In light of the difficulty in obtaining a legal finding of obscenity, local communities have sought to restrict centers of adult entertainment through the use of zoning ordinances. The effectiveness as well as the constitutionality of such ordinances will be addressed in this chapter.

It is commonly understood that municipalities are granted broad zoning power to enhance the quality of life in their communities. However, when zoning ordinances infringe upon constitutional rights, such action must be closely scrutinized by the courts. Only narrowly drawn ordinances with justified objectives will be upheld. Over the past ten years various communities have sought to limit the operation of adult entertainment centers in a way that the Constitution and the courts will accept.

The key case on the issue is Young v. American Mini Theatres, 427 U.S. 50 (1976). In Young, the U.S. Supreme Court upheld the constitutionality of a Detroit ordinance that regulated adult entertainment. Specifically, on November 2, 1972, Detroit enacted zoning ordinances that prohibited an adult facility from locating less than one thousand feet from any two other adult facilities. The Detroit Council made the determination that a concentration of adult centers led to the "downgrading" of neighborhoods. The operators of two adult film theatres challenged the ordinances as an unconstitutional prior restraint of free speech and violative of equal protection.

The District Court for the Eastern District of Michigan dismissed the complaint, holding the ordinances were a "rational attempt to preserve the city's neighborhoods." On appeal, however, the Circuit Court of Appeals reversed concluding that the ordinances were a prior restraint on constitutionally protected speech.

The U.S. Supreme Court reversed the Court of Appeals and upheld the constitutionality of the statute. The Court concluded that the ordinances did not necessarily restrict access to adult entertainment centers, and therefore did not suppress constitutionally protected speech. The Court wrote:

> The situation would be quite different if the ordinance had the effect of suppressing, or greatly restricting access to, lawful speech. Here, however, the District Court specifically found that '[t]he Ordinances do not affect the operation of existing establishments but only the location of new ones. There are myriad locations in the City of Detroit which must be over 1000 feet from existing regulated establishments. This burden on First Amendment rights is slight.'

Additionally, the Court also agreed with the city that a concentration of adult entertainment centers "cause the area to deteriorate and become a focus of crime." This factor further reinforced the city's right to enact such a law.

The Young decision essentially applied a two part test for determining the constitutionality of an ordinance aimed at curbing the use of pornography. First, it must be shown that there is a reason for enacting the law. Second, it must be shown that the law is narrowly drawn to infringe upon the least amount of protected speech. Justice Powell in his concurring opinion, elaborated on the test as follows:

> [A] government regulation is sufficiently justified, despite its incidental impact upon First Amendment interest, 'if it is within the constitutional power of the Government; if it furthers an important or substantial governmental interest; if the governmental interest is unrelated to the suppression of free expression; and if the incidental restriction on First Amendment Freedoms is no greater than is essential to the furtherance of that interest.'

Only if a local ordinance could satisfy these elements can it withstand constitutional scrutiny.

Communities throughout the country interpreted the Young decision as approving zoning ordinances to prohibit adult entertainment. Many were quick to enact their own laws. Some communities, however, acted too quickly and wound up in court unable to defend their laws. Although courts have recognized a community's interest in maintaining the integrity of its neighborhoods, such courts will not permit communities to enact what amounts to a blanket ban on adult entertainment centers.

In Alexander v. City of Minneapolis, 698 F.2d 936 (1983), Minneapolis enacted an ordinance to regulate adult entertainment centers. The ordinance prohibited an adults-only facility from operating within five hundred feet of a residentially zoned district, church, day care facility or educational facility. The law also prohibited the operation of an adults-only facility from operating within five hundred feet of another facility.

Both the Federal District Court and Circuit Court found that under the Minneapolis law all the theatres were in prohibited areas. The courts found that as many as nine out of the ten adult bookstores in the city were also in prohibited areas. Even if the stores and theatres tried to relocate, the courts noted that there were not enough new legal sites to accommodate them. Both courts agreed:

> [E]nforcement of [the ordinance] would have the effect of substantially reducing the number of adult bookstores and theatres in Minneapolis, and no new adult bookstores or theatres would be able to open.

With these factors in mind it was clear that the purpose of the Minneapolis ordinance was to eliminate public access to sexually oriented (but non-obscene) adult entertainment. As the Supreme Court pointed out in Young, the First Amendment could not tolerate such a restriction. As long as material is not obscene it is constitutionally protected, and those wishing to view it must be permitted access.

Commercial Viability

The Alexander decision struck down local ordinances that did not provide for other economically viable sites for an adult entertainment center to relocate. This concept has come to be known as the "commercial viability" factor. If a particular ordinance forces an adult facility to move, it must provide for other commercially economical areas for that facility to relocate. For example, to be successful an adult facility should be located in a business area that is well lighted and close to traffic. Local ordinances must provide for adult facilities to operate in these areas otherwise the access requirement in Young and its later cases will not be satisfied.

Harmful Effects

Finally, the issue of justification for zoning adult entertainment must be addressed. Recent cases require that a community give factual evidence showing the harmful effects of adult facilities on neighborhoods and their children. Communities must also be able to show that an ordinance restricting the operation of these facilities will lessen the problem. One District Court noted that in some cases the justifications for eliminating adult facilities is very real:

> (l) adult book stores cause decreases in property values;
>
> (2) strangers filter into the communities located near such establishments, which cause residents to feel unsafe;
>
> (3) book store patrons park their cars on neighborhood streets which cause parking problems;

(4) men are seen urinating and masturbating in the parking lots;

(5) trash, especially beer cans, is thrown from parking lots onto residential property; and

(6) automobiles and trucks of book store patrons are directly involved in accidents with residents.

If these factors can be established, the need for zoning ordinances will appear quite compelling. Furthermore, if children live in these areas or must pass through them on their way to school, then the need for zoning regulations may be indispensable.

In short, Young and its progeny establish that adult facilities pose a threat to the integrity of neighborhoods. However, in restricting this threat, communities must be careful not to suppress protected speech. Those wishing to view adult material must be permitted unhindered access to such facilities. Only by drawing ordinances to satisfy these two ends may a law be found constitutional.

Chapter 12
TELEPHONE "PORNOGRAPHY"

The use of the telephone to harass and annoy the public has been a serious problem for many years. As a result, both Congress and the states have enacted laws prohibiting such conduct. Despite these laws, the use of obscene and pornographic language on the telephone has skyrocketed. Where such language was once limited to private quarters as an annoyance, it has recently become a highly popular commercial enterprise. This chapter will first address state and federal laws that prohibit the use of obscene or indecent language on the telephone to annoy others. Next, it will concentrate on a new law enacted by Congress to curb the use of commercial telephone sex services.

In 1976 Congress enacted a statute prohibiting obscene or harassing phone calls. 47 U.S.C. §223 reads as follows:

> Whoever --
>
> (l) in the District of Columbia or in interstate or foreign communication by means of telephone --

(A) makes any comment, request, suggestion or proposal which is obscene, lewd, lascivious, filthy, or indecent;

(B) makes a telephone call, whether or not conversation ensues, without disclosing his identity and with intent to annoy, abuse, threaten, or harass any person at the called number;

(C) makes or causes the telephone of another repeatedly or continually to ring, with intent to harass any person at the called number; or

(D) makes repeated telephone calls, during which conversation ensues, solely to harass any person at the called number;

shall be fined not more than $500 or imprisoned not more than six months or both.

The constitutionality of this federal statute, as well as the various state statutes, has been frequently challenged, usually on the ground that it is overbroad on its face. This is of course a First Amendment attack. Both state and federal courts have rejected these challenges because they hold that the government has a compelling interest in the protection of innocent individuals from fear, abuse or annoyance by persons who employed the telephone, not to <u>communicate</u>, but for other unjustifiable motives. That compelling interest is unrelated to the suppression of free expression. The specific intent requirement in the statutes "precludes the proscription of mere communication." In short, such statutes regulate <u>conduct</u>, not mere speech.

In one state case, the court said: "A recital on the telephone of the most sublime prayer with the intention and effect of harassing the listener would fall within its ban as readily as the most scurrilous epithet." Indeed, by its express terms the statute may be violated where no conversation at all occurs.

The courts are noting that harassing telephone calls are an unwarranted invasion of privacy. The "possible chilling effect on free speech. . ." of the statutes strike the courts "as mild compared with the all-too-prevalent and widespread misuse of the telephone to hurt others. The risk that the (statutes) will chill people from, or prosecute them for, the exercise of free speech is remote. The evil against which the statutes are directed is both real and ugly."

But our interest in this volume focuses on the issue of obscenity prohibition in such legislation. Recently the Federal Communications Commission solicited public comment about how it could enforce a new law that declares illegal any commercial telephone sex service featuring "obscene or indecent" language if it is available to minors. The law, sponsored by Representative Thomas J. Bliley, Jr., a Republican of Virginia, and signed by President Reagan in December, 1983, was prompted by Mr. Bliley's displeasure over the commission's refusal to block a New York telephone sex service operated by the publishers of High Society, a magazine featuring sexually explicit photographs.

The law requires the FCC to set standards for determining when a telephone sex service has taken reasonable steps to block access by minors. In such a case, the phone service is immune from prosecution.

The commission received advice from dozens of parties beyond members of the general public.

The American Legal Foundation, a conservative Washington public-interest law firm, said it saw nothing wrong with a prohibition on the operation of such services in daytime hours when children were away from home and thus from parental supervision. They also recommended blocking calls to such services from pay phones.

The American Civil Liberties Union responded that both proposals would unavoidably "infringe on the rights of adults to freely call a service."

Telephone companies told the Commission that they could not be expected to act as censors, determining in advance what was and was not legally obscene.

The provision is an amendment to 47 U.S.C. §223, quoted in the beginning of this chapter. How this curb on telephone pornography will ultimately be interpreted and whether it will hold up constitutionally, remains an open question at this time.

The full amendment reads as follows:

> SEC. 8 (a) Section 223 of the Communications Act of 1934 (47 U.S.C. §223) is amended --
>
> (b)(1) Whoever knowingly --
>
> (A) in the District of Columbia or in interstate or foreign communication, by telephone, makes (directly or by recording device) any obscene or indecent communication for commercial purposes to any person under eighteen years of age or to any other person without that person's consent, regardless of whether the

maker of such communication placed the call; or

(B) permits any telephone facility under such person's control to be used for an activity prohibited by subparagraph (A), shall be fined not more than $50,000 or imprisoned not more than six months, or both.

Although the new law may seem harsh, it also provides that a telephone sex service operator will not be convicted if he can show that he complied with FCC regulations. The FCC is expected to set forth regulations for the new law in June of 1984.

Chapter 13
CONCLUSION

Several years ago sex related businesses such as adult bookstores, massage parlors, and movie theatres were linked only to sleazy city neighborhoods. Now, however, the sex industry has skyrocketed into what government sources say is at least a 4 billion dollar industry. X-rated video cassettes, erotic cable television programs, private sex clubs and erotic boutiques are evidence of the industry's expansion. There is every reason to believe that the industry will continue to grow at an accelerated rate.

In 1973 the Supreme Court set forth its famous Miller obscenity test, which established protected speech and unprotected obscenity. Applying the test, most government officials have found it difficult, if not impossible, to limit pornography. Nowadays under the Miller test rarely, if ever, is a book, film, or magazine found obscene. For this reason, pornography currently pervades many areas of American Society.

Supporters of pornography cling to the First Amendment for protection. They claim that to prohibit pornography would deprive people of their First Amendment rights. It would also deprive others of their right to view pornography. More important, banning pornography would give the government a power of censorship, something history tells us has a great potential for abuse. For example, prior to the Roth decision in 1957 states banned dozens of movies simply because they were "immoral" or not in the public interest. Supporters of pornography claim that to again give federal and state governments the power of censorship would inevitably lead to the suppression of constitutionally protected speech and ideas. At bottom, by permitting pornography the courts have chosen the lesser of two evils.

But opponents of pornography believe the greater evil lies in pornography. As one writer stated in the March, 1984 issue of Time:

> The ordinary person, of course, does not need a philosopher, conservative or otherwise, to tell him why he wants to run pornography out of his neighborhood. It cheapens and demeans. Even though he may occasionally be tempted by it, that temptation is almost invariably accompanied by a feeling of shame and a desire to shield his children

from the fleshy come-ons of the magazine rack.

For this reason, many believe there is a compelling state interest in eliminating pornography, which outweighs the commands of the First Amendment. Not surprisingly, opponents of pornography generally believe the Supreme Court's efforts in the field have been a failure.

Nevertheless, opponents of pornography have won some recent victories in the courts. These victories were won not by proving certain pornographic materials obscene, but rather by proving that certain pornographic materials are easily accessible to children. The Pacifica decision, for example, ensures that commercial television and radio will be kept free from indecent programming. Unless cable television companies can provide suitable means for preventing children from viewing erotic programs, i.e., with lockboxes and late-night scheduling, Pacifica may one day be extended to cover cable television as well. Courts have also permitted states to prohibit child pornography whether or not it is obscene. Finally, in some instances, courts are beginning to allow communities to zone out adult entertainment centers where such centers present a threat to the integrity of neighborhoods and their children.

The net result of this discussion essentially is that as long as children are not involved, courts will generally strive to permit the publication or exhibition of pornographic material. However, when children are involved, courts will strive to ban the material. Apparently, courts are no longer concerned with adults and pornography. It is only the possible adverse effects of pornography upon children which will outweigh the First Amendment. There is nothing new in this theory. Over ten years ago Justice Brennan, in his dissent in Paris Adult Theatre v. Slaton, advocated such a position as a reasonable balance between those who oppose pornography and the First Amendment.

APPENDIXES

Appendix A
Table of Cases

Alexander v. City of Minneapolis
698 F.2d 936 (8th cir. 1983)

Bantam Books v. Sullivan
372 U.S. 58 (1963)

Burstyn v. Wilson
343 U.S. 495 (1952)

Chaplinsky v. New Hampshire
315 U.S. 568 (1942)

Commonwealth v. Fried
271 Mass. 318 (1930)

Cruz v. Ferre
571 F.Supp. 125 (S.D. Fla. 1983)

FCC v. Pacifica
438 U.S. 776 (1978)

Freedman v. Maryland
380 U.S. 51 (1965)

Ginsberg v. New York
390 U.S. 629 (1968)

Ginzberg v. New York
383 U.S. 463 (1965)

HBO v. Wilkinson
581 F.Supp. 936 (D. Utah 1982)

Jacobellis v. Ohio
378 U.S. 184 (1964)

Kaplan v. California
413 U.S. 115 (1973)

Kingsley Picture Corp. v. Regents
360 U.S. 684 (1959)

Manual Enterprises v. Day
370 U.S. 478 (1962)

Memoirs v. Massachusetts
383 U.S. 413 (1965)

Miller v. California
413 U.S. 15 (1973)

Mishkin v. New York
383 U.S. 502 (1966)

Mutual Film Corp. v. Industrial Comm.
236 U.S. 230 (1915)

Paris Adult Theatre v. Slaton
413 U.S. 49 (1973)

People v. Dial Press
182 Misc. 416 (1944)

Red Lion Broadcasting v. FCC
395 U.S. 367 (1968)

Regina v. Hicklin
L.R. 3 Queens Bench 36

Roth v. United States
354 U.S. 476 (1957)

Stanley v. Georgia
394 U.S. 557 (1969)

Times Film Corp. v. Chicago
365 U.S. 43 (1961)

United States v. Kennerly
209 F. 119 (1913)

United States v. One Book Entitled Ulysses
5 F.Supp. 182 (1933)

Young v. Americana Mini Theatres
427 U.S. 50 (1976)

Appendix B
Federal Statutes Prohibiting Obscenity

(18 U.S.C. §1461-1465)

§1461. Mailing obscene or crime-inciting matter

Every obscene, lewd, lascivious, indecent, filthy or vile article, matter, thing, device, or substance; and --

Every article or thing designed, adapted, or intended for producing abortion, or for any indecent or immoral use; and

Every article, instrument, substance, drug, medicine or thing which is advertised or described in a manner calculated to lead another to use or apply it for producing abortion, or for any indecent or immoral purpose; and

Every written or printed card, letter, circular, book, pamphlet, advertisement, or notice of any kind giving information, directly or indirectly, where, or how, or from whom, or by what means any of such mentioned matters, articles, or things may be obtained or made, or where or by whom any act or operation of any kind for the procuring or producing of abortion will be done or performed, or how or by what means abortion may be produced, whether sealed or unsealed; and

Every paper, writing, advertisement, or representation that any article, instrument, substance, drug, medicine, or thing may, or can, be used or applied for producing abortion, or for any indecent or immoral purpose; and

Every description calculated to induce or incite a person to so use or apply any such article, instrument, substance, drug, medicine, or thing --

It declared to be nonmailable matter and shall not be conveyed in the mails or delivered from any post office or by any letter carrier.

Whoever knowingly uses the mails for the mailing, carriage in the mails, or delivery of anything declared by this section or section 3001(e) of title 39 [39 USC §3001(e)] to be nonmailable, or knowingly causes to be delivered by mail according to the direction thereon, or at the place at which it is directed to be delivered by the person to whom it is addressed, or knowingly takes any such thing from the mails for the purpose of circulating or disposing thereof, or of aiding in the circulation of disposition thereof, shall be fined not more than $5,000 or imprisoned not more than five years, or both, for the first such offense, and shall be fined not more than $10,000 or imprisoned not more than ten years, or both, for each such offense thereafter.

The term "indecent," as used in this section includes matter of a character tending to incite arson, murder, or assassination.

§1462. Importation or transportation of obscene matters

Whoever brings into the United States, or any place subject to the jurisdiction thereof, or knowingly uses any express company or other common carrier, or carriage in interstate or foreign commerce --

(a) any obscene, lewd, lascivious, or filthy book, pamphlet, picture, motion-picture film, paper, letter, writing, print, or other matter of indecent character; or

(b) any obscene, lewd, lascivious, or filthy phonograph recording, electrical transcription, or other article or thing capable of producing sound; or

(c) any drug, medicine, article or thing designed, adapted, or intended for producing abortion, or for any indecent or immoral use; or any written or printed card, letter, circular, book, pamphlet, advertisement, or notice of any kind giving information directly or indirectly, where, how, or of whom, or by what means any of such mentioned articles, matters, or things may be obtained or made; or

Whoever knowingly takes from such express company or other common carrier any matter or thing the carriage of which is herein made unlawful --

Shall be fined not more than $5,000 or imprisoned not more than five years, or both, for the first offense and shall be fined not more than $10,000 or imprisoned not more than ten years, or both, for each such offense thereafter.

§1465. Transportation of obscene matters for sale or distribution.

Whoever knowingly transports in interstate or foreign commerce for the purpose of sale or distribution any obscene, lewd, lascivious, or filthy book, pamphlet, picture, film, paper, letter, writing, print, silhouette, drawing, figure, image, cast, phonograph recording, electrical transcription or other article capable of producing sound or any other matter of indecent or immoral character, shall be fined not more than $5,000 or imprisoned not more than five years, or both.

The transportation as aforesaid of two or more copies of any publication or two or more of any article of the character described above, or a combined total of five such publications and articles, shall create a presumption that such publications or articles are intended for sale or distribution, but such presumption shall be rebuttable.

Why any person is convicted of a violation of this Act, the court in its judgment of conviction may, in addition to the penalty prescribed, order the confiscation and disposal of such items described herein which were found in the possession or under the immediate control of such person at the time of his arrest.

§1464. Broadcasting obscene language.

Whoever utters any obscene, indecent, or profane language by means of radio communcation shall be fined not more than $10,000 or imprisoned not more than two years, or both.

§1463. Mailing indecent matter on wrappers or envelopes.

All matter otherwise mailable by law, upon the envelope or outside cover or wrapper of which, and all postal cards upon which, any delineations, epithets, terms, or language of an indecent, lewd, lascivious, or obscene character are written or printed or otherwise impressed or apparent, are nonmailable matter, and shall not be conveyed in the mails nor delivered from any post office nor by any letter carrier, and shall be withdrawn from the mails under such regulations as the Postal Service shall prescribe.

Whoever knowingly deposits for mailing or delivery, anything declared by this section to be nonmailable matter, or knowingly takes the same from the mails for the purpose of circulating or disposing of or aiding in the circulation or disposition of the same, shall be fined not more than $5,000 or imprisoned not more than five years, or both.

Appendix C
States Which Have Adopted or Judicially Incorporated the *Miller* Test for Obscenity

Alabama	13A-12-150
Arizona	13-3501(2)
Arkansas	41-3502(6)
Colorado	18-7-101(2)
Delaware	11, §1364
Georgia	26-2101(b)
Hawaii	712-1201(6)
Idaho	18-4101(A)
Iowa	728.4
Indiana	35-30-10.1-1(c)
Kansas	21-4301(2)(a)
Kentucky	531.010(3)
Louisiana	14:106(A)(2)
Maryland	Ebert v. State Bd. of Censors, 313 A.2d 536 (1973)
Massachusetts	272, §31
Michigan	People v. Neumayer, 275 N.W.2d 230 (1979)
Minnesota	State v. Welke, 216 N.W.2d 641 (1974)
Missouri	573.010(1)
Nebraska	28-807(a)
Nevada	201.235
New Hampshire	650:1 (IV)
New Jersey	20:34-2
New York	Penal 235

North Carolina	14-190.1(b)
North Dakota	12.1-27.1-01(4)
Ohio	State v. Burgur, 384 N.E.2d 255 (1978)
Oklahoma	McCrary v. State, 533 P.2d 629 (1974)
Oregon	167.087(2)
Pennsylvania	18, §5903(b)
Rhode Island	11-31-1
South Carolina	16-15-260(a)
South Dakota	22-24-27(10)
Tennessee	39-3001(1)
Texas	Penal 43.21(a)
Utah	76-10-1203(1)
Virginia	18.2-372
Washington	184, §1(2)

STATES WHICH CONTINUE TO FOLLOW THE ROTH-MEMOIRS STANDARD

California	Penal 311(a)
Connecticut	53a-193
Florida	847.07
Illinois	11-20(b)

Appendix D
State Child Pornography Statutes

APPENDIX E

STATE CHILD PORNOGRAPHY STATUTES

I. STATE STATUTES WHICH PROHIBIT THE DISSEMINATION OF CHILD PORNOGRAPHIC MATERIAL REGARDLESS OF WHETHER IT IS OBSCENE

Arizona	13-3553
Colorado	18-6-403
Delaware	11-1108
Flordia	847.014
Hawaii	707-751
Kentucky	531.320, 531.340-360
Louisiana	14:81.1(A)(3)
Massachusetts	272, §29A
Michigan	750.145(c)(3)
Mississippi	97-5-33(4)
Montana	45-5-625
New Jersey	2C:24-4(b)(5)
New York	Penal 263
Oklahoma	21, §1021.2
Pennsylvania	18, §6312(c)
Rhode Island	41-9-1.1
Texas	Penal 43.25
Utah	76-10-1206.5(3)
West Virginia	61-8c-3
Wisconsin	940.203(4)

2. STATES WHICH PROHIBIT THE DISSEMINATION OF CHILD PORNOGRAPHIC MATERIAL ONLY IF IT IS OBSCENE.

Alabama	13-7-231, 232
Arkansas	41-4204
California	Penal 311.2(b)
Illinois	38, 11-20a(b)(1)
Indiana	35-30-10.1-2
Maine	17, §2923(1)
Minnesota	617.246(3) & (4)
Nebraska	28-1463(2)
New Hampshire	650:2 (II)
North Dakota	12.1-27.1-01
Ohio	2907.321(A)
Oregon	163.485
South Dakota	22-22-24, 25
Tennessee	39-1020
Washington	9.68A.030
Federal Statute	18 U.S.C. 2252

3. STATES WHICH PROHIBIT THE USE OF MINORS IN PORNOGRAPHIC MATERIAL.

Alaska	11.41.455
Georgia	26-9943a(b)
Idaho	44-1306
Iowa	728.12

Kansas	21-3516
Maryland	27, §419A
Missouri	568.060
Nevada	200.509
New Mexico	30-6-1
North Carolina	14-190.6
South Carolina	16-15-380
Wyoming	14-3-102(a)(v)(E)

4. STATES WHICH REGULATE ONLY THE DISTRIBUTION OF PORNOGRAPHIC MATERIALS TO MINORS.

Maine	17, §2911
Montana	45-8-201
New Mexico	30-37-2
Vermont	13, §2802
West Virginia	61-8A-2

Appendix E
Federal Child Pornography Statutes
(18 U.S.C. 2251-2253)

§ 2251. Sexual exploitation of children

(a) Any person who employs, uses, persuades, induces, entices, or coerces any minor to engage in, or who has a minor assist any other person to engage in, any sexually explicit conduct for the purpose of producing any visual or print medium depicting such conduct, shall be punished as provided under subsection (c), if such person knows or has reason to know that such visual or print medium will be transported in interstate or foreign commerce or mailed, or if such visual or print medium has actually been transported in interstate or foreign commerce or mailed.

(b) Any parent, legal guardian, or person having custody or control of a minor who knowingly permits such minor to engage in, or to assist any other person to engage in, sexually explicit conduct for the purpose of producing any visual or print medium depicting such conduct shall be punished as provided under subsection (c) of this section, if such parent, legal guardian, or person knows or has reason to know that such visual or print medium will be transported in interstate or foreign commerce or mailed or if such visual or print medium has actually been transported in interstate or foreign commerce or mailed.

(c) Any person who violates this section shall be fined not more than $10,000, or imprisoned not more than 10 years, or both, but, if such person has a prior conviction under this section, such person shall be fined not more than $15,000, or imprisoned not less than two years nor more than 15 years, or both.

§ 2252. Certain activities relating to material involving the sexual exploitation of minors

(a) Any person who—

(1) knowingly transports or ships in interstate or foreign commerce or mails, for the purpose of sale or distribution for sale, any obscene visual or print medium, if—

(A) the producing of such visual or print medium involves the use of a minor engaging in sexually explicit conduct; and

(B) such visual or print medium depicts such conduct; or

(2) knowingly receives for the purpose of sale or distribution for sale, or knowingly sells or distributes for sale, any obscene visual or print medium that has been transported or shipped in interstate or foreign commerce or mailed, if—

(A) the producing of such visual or print medium involves the use of a minor engaging in sexually explicit conduct; and

(B) such visual or print medium depicts such conduct;

shall be punished as provided in subsection (b) of this section.

(b) Any person who violates this section shall be fined not more than $10,000, or imprisoned not more than 10 years, or both, but, if such person has a prior conviction under this section, such person shall be fined not more than $15,000, or imprisoned not less than two years nor more than 15 years, or both.

§ 2253. Definitions for chapter

For the purposes of this chapter, the term—

(1) "minor" means any person under the age of sixteen years;

(2) "sexually explicit conduct" means actual or simulated—

(A) sexual intercourse, including genital-genital, oral-genital, anal-genital, or anal-anal, whether between persons of the same or opposite sex;

(B) bestiality;

(C) masturbation;

(D) sado-masochistic abuse (for the purpose of sexual stimulation); or

(E) lewd exhibition of the genitals or pubic area of any person;

(3) "producing" means producing, directing, manufacturing, issuing, publishing, or advertising, for pecuniary profit; and

(4) "visual or print medium" means any film, photograph, negative, slide, book, magazine, or other visual or print medium.

Appendix F
Movies Banned in the U.S. Since 1908
(Source: *Banned Films:* Grazia & Newman, R.R. Bowker Corp. 1982)

1908–1919

1 The James Boys in Missouri
2 Night Riders
3 The Birth of a Nation
4 The Ordeal
5 Willard-Johnson Boxing Match
6 Birth Control
7 The Hand That Rocks the Cradle

8 The Sex Lure
9 The Spirit of '76
10 The Spy
11 The Easiest Way
12 The Brand
13 Fit to Win

1920–1939

14 Newsreels
15 The Naked Truth
16 Alibi
17 The Road to Ruin
18 Ecstasy
19 The Youth of Maxim
20 Spain in Flames
21 Tomorrow's Children
22 The Birth of a Baby
23 Professor Mamlock
24 Remous

1940–1959

25 Victory in the West
26 The Outlaw
27 Amok
28 Mom and Dad
29 Curley
30 The Miracle
31 La Ronde
32 Latuko
33 M
34 Miss Julie
35 Pinky
36 The Moon Is Blue
37 Native Son
38 Baby Doll
39 The Game of Love
40 The Garden of Eden
41 The Man with the Golden Arm
42 Wild Weed
43 Lady Chatterley's Lover
44 Naked Amazon
45 And God Created Woman
46 The Anatomy of a Murder
47 Desire Under the Elms
48 Don Juan
49 The Lovers

1960–1969

50 Never on Sunday
51 The Connection
52 The Virgin Spring
53 Women of the World
54 Bachelor Tom Peeping
55 491
56 Have Figure Will Travel

57 Lorna
58 Revenge at Daybreak
59 A Stranger Knocks
60 The Twilight Girls
61 The Bedford Incident
62 Bunny Lake Is Missing
63 The Dirty Girls
64 The Unsatisfied
65 Un Chant d'Amour
66 This Picture Is Censored
67 Viva Maria
68 A Woman's Urge
69 Body of a Female
70 I, a Woman
71 I Am Curious—Yellow
72 Mondo Freudo
73 Rent-a-Girl
74 Alimony Lovers
75 Carmen, Baby
76 The Female
77 The Fox
78 Therese and Isabelle
79 Titicut Follies
80 The Wicked Die Slow
81 Angelique in Black Leather
82 Blue Movie
83 Candy
84 The Language of Love
85 Odd Triangle
86 Pattern of Evil
87 Yellow Bird

1970–1981

88 The Collection
89 The Libertine
90 The Secret Sex Lives of Romeo and Juliet

91 Starlet
92 The Vixen
93 Where Eagles Dare
94 Without a Stitch
95 Woodstock
96 The Art of Marriage
97 Cindy and Donna
98 Computer Game
99 It All Comes Out in the End
100 The Killing of Sister George
101 Lysistrata
102 Magic Mirror
103 Pornography in Denmark
104 Sexual Freedom in Denmark
105 Carnal Knowledge
106 Cry Uncle
107 Deep Throat
108 Sinderella
109 Behind the Green Door
110 The Exorcist
111 The Last Picture Show
112 Last Tango in Paris
113 The Newcomers
114 Class of '74
115 School Girl
116 Stewardesses
117 The Devil in Miss Jones
118 Gun Runners
119 I Am Sandra
120 Naked Came the Stranger
121 Caligula
122 Emmanuelle

Appendix G
Model Cable Pornography Statute
(Proposed By Morality in Media)

Section 1

(a) No person (including franchisee) shall by means of a cable television system, knowingly distribute by wire or cable to its subscribers any indecent material or knowingly provide such material for distribution.

(b) "Person" shall include individuals, partnerships, associations and corporations.

(c) "distribute" shall mean send, transmit or retransmit or otherwise pass through a cable television system.

(d) "Material" means any visual material shown on a cable television system, whether or not accompanied by a soundtrack, or any sound recording played on a cable television system.

(e) "Indecent material" shall mean material which is a representation or verbal description of:

1. a human sexual or excretory organ or function; or
2. nudity; or
3. ultimate sexual acts, normal or perverted, actual or simulated; or
4. masturbation;

which under contemporary community standards for cable television is patently offensive.

(f) "Community Standards" shall mean the standards of the community encompassed within the territorial area covered by the franchise.

(g) "Provide" means to supply for use.

(h) "A person acts knowingly" if he has knowledge of the character or nature of the material involved. A person is presumed to have knowledge of the character or nature of the material if he has actual notice of the nature of such material whether or not he has precise notice of its contents.

Section 2

Violation of this statute shall constitute a misdemeanor and any person convicted of such violation shall be confined in jail for not more than ____________ months or fined not more than ____________ Dollars, either or both.

Appendix H
Suggestions for Further Reading

Articles on Roth v. U.S.

Henkin. Morals and the Constitution: The Sin of Obscenity. 63 Columbia L. Rev. 391 (1963).

Lockhat and McClure. Censorship of Obscenity: The Developing Constitutional Standards. 45 Minn. L. Rev. 1 (1960).

Note. Obscenity and the Supreme Court: Nine Years of Confusion. 19 Stan. L. Rev. 167 (1966).

Post Roth Articles

Magrath. The Obscenity Cases: Grapes of Roth. 1966 Supreme Court Review.

Note. More Ado About Dirty Books. 75 Yale Law Journal 1364 (1966).

Articles on the 1973 Decision

Clor. Obscenity and the First Amendment: Round Three. 7 Loyola U. L. Rev. (L.A.) 207 (1974).

Fahringer and Brown. Rise and Fall of Roth - A Critique of the Recent Supreme Court Obscenity Decisions. 10 Crim. L. Bull. 735 (1974).

Hunsaker. 1983 Obscenity-Pornography Decisions: Analysis, Impact, and Legislative Alternatives. 11 S. Diego L. Rev. 906 (1974).

Note. Obscenity '73: Something Old, A Little Bit New, Quite a Bit Borrowed, But Nothing Blue. 33 Md. L. Rev. 421 (1973).

Child Pornography

Case Notes on New York v. Ferber:

19 Suffolk U. L. Rev. 96 (1983)
19 Wake Forest L. Rev. 95 (1983)
28 Villanova L. Rev. 416 (1983)
7 Journal of Juvenile Law 180 (1983)
13 Golden Gate U.L. Rev. 475 (1983)

Moore. Child Pornography, The First Amendment, and The Media: The Constitutionality of Super Obscenity Laws. 4 Comment 15 (1981).

See No Evil, Speak No Evil, Read No Evil: The Child v. The First Amendment. 4 Child. Legal Rights Journal 20, (1982).

<u>Media and Pornography</u>

Drysdale. Indecency and the First Amendment: Special Problems of the Broadcast Industry. 13 *Lincoln L. Rev.* 101, 1982.

Faines. Obscenity, Cable Television and the First Amendment: Will F.C.C. Regulation Impair the Market Place of Ideas? 21 *Duquesne L. Rev.* 965 1983.

Hanks and Coran. Federal Preemption of State Obscenity Law Applied to Broadcasting. 5 Comment 21 (1982).

Hofbauer. "Cableporn" and the First Amendment: Perspectives on Content Regulation of Cable Television. 35 *Fed. Comm. L.J.* 139 (1983).

Indecent Programming on Cable Television and the First Amendment. 51 *George Washington L. Rev.* 254 (1983).

Nichols. Vulgarity and Obscenity in the Student Press. 10 *Journal of Law and Education* 207 1981.

Pignanelli. Regulation and Indecent Television Programming. 9 *Journal of Contemporary Law* 207 (1983).

Sociological Aspects

Ben-Veniste. Pornography and Sex Crime: The Danish Experience. 7 Technical Report of the Commission on Obscenity and Pornography, 245 (1971).

Daniels. The Supreme Court and Obscenity: An Exercise in Empirical Constitutional Policy-Making, 17 San Diego L. Rev. 757 (1980).

Herrman and Bordner. Attitudes Toward Pornography in a Southern Community. 21 Criminology 349 (1983).

Kercher & Walker. Reactions of Convicted Rapists to Sexually Explicit Stimuli. 81 Journal of Abnormal Psychology 46 (1973).

Ursel. Pornography and Violence. 54 Obiter Dicta (1982).

Nuisance Statutes

Albaugh. Regulation of Obscenity through Nusiance Statutes and Injustice Remedies, the Prior Restraint Dilemma. 19 Wake Forest L. Rev. 7 (1983).

Burns. Zoning Prohibition Which Impinges on First Amendment Activity Must be Adequately Justified By Municipality. 12 Seton Hall L. Rev. 311 (1982).

Control of Obscenity Through Enforcement of a Nuisance Statute. 4 Campbell L. Rev. 139 (1981).

Lupo. Prior Restraint of Obscenity as a Public Nuisance. 26 New York Law School L. Rev. 1122, 1981.

Pearson. State Regulation of Obscene Motion Pictures: The Red Light Nuisance Statute. 31 Alabama L. Rev. 274 (1980).

Books

Clor. Obscenity and Public Morality. University of Chicago Press (1969).

Degruzia and Newman. Banned Films: Movies, Censors and the First Amendment. R.R. Bowker Comp. (1982).

Schauer. The Law of Obscenity, Bureau of National Affairs (1976).

Sobel. Pornography, Obscenity and the Law. Checkmark Books (1979).

Sunderland. _Obscenity: The Court, the Congress, and the President's Commission_. Domestic Affairs Studies (1975).

INDEX

DUE DATE
